# STORY
# DRAMA

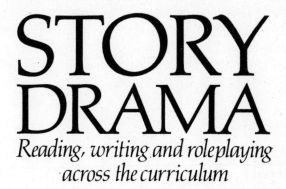

# STORY DRAMA
### Reading, writing and roleplaying across the curriculum

## David Booth

Pembroke Publishers Limited

© 1994 Pembroke Publishers
     538 Hood Road
     Markham, Ontario L3R 3K9

**Canadian Cataloguing in Publication Data**

Booth, David,
  Story drama: reading, writing, and role-playing
across the curriculum

Includes bibliographical references and index.
ISBN 1-55138-038-2

1. Drama in education.  2. Language arts – Correlation
with content subjects.  I. Title.

PN3171.B66 1994    372.13'32    C94-931828-0


Editor: David Kilgour
Design: John Zehethofer
Cover Photography: Ajay Photographics
Front Cover Background: Judith Welbourn
Typesetting: Jay Tee Graphics Ltd.

This book was produced with the generous assistance of the government of Ontario through the Ministry of Culture, Tourism and Recreation.


Printed and bound in Canada by Webcom
9 8 7 6 5 4 3 2 1

# Contents

# Introduction

Dear Mr. Booth:

You are a funny person and you are a good actress.

Danny, Grade One

When I began teaching fifth grade in Hamilton, Ontario, I knew little about drama, except for the occasional high school production in which I'd been someone in the chorus. That year I taught my class a few parodies involving Captain Cook and Columbus and took part in the spring festival with a campy retelling of Cinderella, aided by folk dances created by the physical education consultant.

However, during my second year, Bill Moore, my supervisor in oral English, stopped me in the playground one day and asked me if I would consider teaching drama to senior public students. Well, I accepted the offer and thus began my apprenticeship with Bill. He had me read thousands of poems and plays and join the Hamilton Players' Guild Amateur Theatre, and he began to awaken in me a love of and appreciation for the power of theatre. In my work at McMaster University toward my B.A. degree, I began taking as many courses as I could in theatre, theatre history, English literature, and poetry, and gradually my grounding in drama deepened.

When I taught drama to grades seven and eight, my basic problem was survival. Five hundred and sixty pupils each week, eight

periods a day, one half-hour spare period a week, one performance required every other Friday. Surviving meant two things
— finding enough material for the drama students who literally
gobbled it up, and finding enough performance pieces to please
a hyper-critical principal. Naturally, I had to trust my students
to supply me with much of my material and most of my energy.
"Skit" seemed to remain the only answer. I knew in my heart
it was wrong; I knew it was a destructive pattern of behavior
for the children — the laughs were cheap, the characters were
stereotyped, the jokes were archaic and unoriginal, the insensitivity of the class was frightening. But I kept telling myself that
this kind of drama was truly educational, that the pupils were
learning *something* and weren't wasting their time. I was wrong,
of course. There were good times: the students gave so much
and perhaps the spirit of the class lifted some of them out of
the drudgery of the junior high years. When reliable drama information arrived on the scene, my lessons collapsed, having been
built on such empty foundations as, "what they think they want
is what they get, regardless of need."

As a drama teacher I was constantly searching for new sources
as we dramatized everything we could find. We sang and spoke
aloud chorally the poems that Bill would give us and anything
that was available in the library or in bookstores. It was a daily
quest to find material that the children could interpret by reading aloud. If only I had understood the nature of drama and had
moved into improvised language, my life would have been so
much easier. In truth there are almost no plays written for children of this age and perhaps there shouldn't be. They need so
much experience understanding themselves and their own lives
that roleplaying should have been the answer all along. I began
taking every workshop and course I could find with educators
such as Brian Way, Richard Courtney, Dorothy Heathcote, Gavin
Bolton, David Kemp and Agnes Buckles, until I began to develop
my own philosophy of what drama in education could be.

I remember the first time I tried whole group drama. It was
with a grade eight gifted class at Dalewood School in Hamilton.
I had just returned from a workshop at Queen's University with
Brian Way, and I thought, "I'm going to try this no matter what."
I put on a record, we moved the desks to the sides of the room,
I told the children to find places by themselves, and I said: "You
are underwater and you're going to find treasure. You are mov-

ing in slow motion as you swim near the wrecks of previous centuries." And what those children did non-verbally with their bodies thrilled me to my core and I suddenly recognized the power of letting the drama emerge from the children's imaginations as opposed to my giving them constant instructions and orders. I never looked back.

During my next few learning years, I discovered what could happen when using drama with young people. Of course, those children whom I had won over originally by promising audience laughter never allowed themselves to be part of the new growth. They were lost to me now. Even slow, gawky Stephen, who had been the butt of so many skits, had grown used to the notoriety — people had laughed when he merely walked to the front of the room. What value could he see in being part of a whole, in exploring relationships, in listening to others so that he could respond honestly and sensitively?

In the sixties, writers began articulating their research and beliefs, and their books supported my own work and led me towards my present-day understanding of the role of drama as a way of learning.

At the same time, I began teaching at a summer school at the University of Toronto where teachers from kindergarten through grade thirteen would come for additional qualification courses in dramatic arts. I really began to question my beliefs, my value system in education, and to piece together almost in a collage fashion my philosophy of drama in education. I was fortunate enough to work with Julianna Saxton and Chuck Lundy in building this department, where we ultimately ran courses for hundreds of teachers in summer and winter evenings in several locations, including England.

As a consultant, I had opportunities to travel in Canada, the United States and Great Britain, taking part in conferences, workshops and seminars, and giving speeches on drama in education. It's amazing how fast you learn when you know very little, how you absorb everything from every speaker, every workshop you attend, every audience that listens. And as you articulate your experiences with children you have worked with, you begin to understand what actually happened.

I participated in week-long seminars in Iowa, London, New York, Vancouver and Winnipeg, and began to develop a scheme for implementing drama with teachers of all age groups. Nothing can equal for me the learning gleaned from discussion with staff at our summer schools or with departmental colleagues as we explored the lessons we had team-taught or collaborated upon, trying to come to grips with things that worked, strategies that had failed and what we could do next.

Over the years, teachers such as David Davis, Howard Reynolds, Wayne Fairhead, Doris Manetta, Ellen Messing, Tony Goode, Jonathan Neelands and Cecily O'Neill have all helped shape my thinking and my work with their deliberations, questions and insights. I have truly felt like an apprentice — and that's what I have been.

In the seventies I was fortunate enough to study with Gavin Bolton at the University of Durham for two years, and his rigor and academic analysis forced me to dig deeply into my own work and to recognize the power of reflective practice. The thesis that Gavin required for my degree led to my writing books wherein the work of the children formed the genesis of my study. From their responses, their ideas, their constructs, I began to shape my own understanding of what drama could achieve.

In my classroom-based projects, I see the same model working so well. Teachers choose their own area of interest and begin to explore it by reflecting on the children's work, taping the children's talk, discussing with the children what happened in their own drama, and generally coming to understand teaching through what has happened in their classrooms. By talking with experts in the field and colleagues, and reading, teachers learn what it is to be a changing teacher, to continue to try to reach each year's students in new and better ways.

My work now consists of using drama in my teaching with undergraduate and graduate student teachers as a means of learning in various curriculum areas. Today, discussing with my own students what the lesson we participated in held for us is my most rewarding activity, and helping those teachers find their own learning is my goal. I'm fortunate to recognize drama's strength and to be able to incorporate its power inside any frame my students have designed. It is indeed a treasure that I have been given, these years of drama, working alongside such committed teachers. These adult learners come from varied backgrounds, most with specialist certificates in one or more educational arts practices, or with experience from the professional arts world. We spend a great deal of time talking about young people and learning, and the participants bring years of observation to bear upon our conversations. However, an over-riding theme that arises every year is the lack of artistic aware-ness and response among the citizens of our communities, even after years of arts education in the schools. What, then, are the arts in education about? And what are the life skills that we want to promote and develop through teaching the arts, through work-ing with drama?

This book is a record of the twenty-five years I have spent work-ing in story drama with children loaned to me by co-operative teachers as demonstration classes, while groups of teachers and student teachers both observed and participated in the experience. Teaching in such a context provided me with oppor-tunities to work with new teachers and teachers new to drama from inside the learning, as we visited schools or brought chil-dren to our drama studio. I find it difficult to believe that so many years have passed, but as I re-read my notes, the children's faces pop into view with each transcript, captured in drama moments. When triggered, I can recall faces and incidents from every group of children with whom I have worked, moments of drama that have seeped into my unconscious and that reappear, seemingly from nowhere, during subsequent teaching encounters. As well, I have had the good fortune to spend hours with teachers after the children had left, discussing the ideas explored, the children's words and phrases, the questions that remained unanswered, the strategies that awaited implementation with the next group.

In my work, story and drama are forever linked. Even now, when I am reviewing a new picture book or novel for children, I cannot escape the possibilities that flood my drama-structured mind. Similarly, when preparing to work with a group of young-sters for the first time in drama, I cannot imagine entering the room without a selection of stories ready to tell or read aloud. Perhaps I require the safety net of narrative in order to attempt the leap into creating stories through drama. Or have I become a storyer, linking incidents and events that the children and I experience together into a narrative that echoes the books and tales that have gone before, connecting the children and me to the story network that gives meaning to our lives? Over the years, I have seen a single tale give rise to a hundred different treat-ments and interpretations, determined by the participants and the moment, each story drama unique, yet included somewhere within the original story's fabric. Occasionally, I still return to the sources I used almost thirty years ago with those wonderful students who for no reason chose to participate and do what I asked, but now I see those selections as sources for so much more than I ever dreamed of at that time. Story drama — which I'll define for the moment as improvised roleplay based on story — surrounds my teaching, and allows children to at once become the co-constructors of a story, the story itself and the characters living within the story: as the poet David McCord says, they are "the singer, the song and the sung."

Teachers need to teach, and children need to be taught by teachers who somehow reflect on what has gone on, so that their future work can be informed and illuminated by past experience. It concerns me deeply that so many educators working in pre-service and in-service courses for teachers no longer work with children. When I was a young teacher, my role models taught children constantly, relating their mistakes and successes, analysing the classroom dynamic, working alongside classroom teachers like me in order to grow in their own understanding of how children learn, at least in a particular situation at one moment in time. I would hope the stories we tell each other about working with children will cause us to change as teachers. We need wise mentors to point the way and guide our reflections, but more than that, we need others who continue to find joy and satisfaction in the struggle to teach, who extend and enrich us with their own explorations, working together.

Over the years, I have noticed a range of styles among teachers, from energetic young apprentices who become the whole drama, leaving children to stare in wonder, to thoughtful practitioners who draw from these young roleplayers concentrated and focused affective thought. Whatever the style or situation, however, story drama can have powerful results. This is worth pointing out because teachers often tell me that they can't replicate my results in the classroom. After all, I appear for a few hours or a few days, armed with plans and stories I have prepared well in advance, and without all the other responsibilities classroom teachers have. "What will the children be like when your novelty wears off?" "You have the time to prepare for one two-hour lesson; we have to keep teaching." And, most often, because I ask the adults observing to work in role whenever possible: "We don't have a bunch of teaching volunteers in our classrooms."

These are valid points, but it is worth noting that any teacher can use story drama to teach, even if it is a rough, improvised session that lasts only a few minutes. Also, a visiting teacher's session can suggest new ideas and approaches, as does any guest's involvement with the children, from an excursion to a gallery, a theatre performance or a trip to the classroom across the hall, to a celebration on parents' night. Children learn all the time in different ways, and a demonstration lesson can give the classroom teacher an opportunity for simply observing the children in a different setting. In every case in which I have participated, the teachers have commented that they have learned something new about one or more of their children.

At times, the classroom teacher is nervous in a public setting with a guest teacher, focused on wanting the children to do well and to feel valued. I remember my first years of teaching, when my language arts supervisor, Bill Moore, would ask if he could work with my class. I would retreat to the back of the room, still controlling each child with invisible threads to be manipulated by me in secret. When I eventually let loose those ties, and relaxed as Bill set free the children into new patterns of behavior, new status roles, new dynamics of interaction, only then did those children emerge into fully rounded human beings for me; it was a bit like watching a Polaroid picture developing over time. On each occasion when Bill Moore visited, I learned more about teaching and more about my children.

When I work with children and teachers, I quickly lose myself in the medium of classroom drama, but the children are front and centre in the learning. Educator Dorothy Heathcote taught me to ensure that those watching not respond as an audience being entertained, but as participants engaged in the struggle to understand the teaching/learning dynamic.

Because of the format of a typical day of demonstration teaching, where we work as a whole group, in small groups, and with partners, teacher-participants can begin to develop their subsequent contributions from the feedback the children give when I draw them together from time to time. The strength and abilities teachers possess never cease to amaze me, and I watch both them and the children, taking direction for the work from their hesitant yet productive interactions. A young teacher once complained to me that during discussions in role, I was not calling upon her for suggestions, and when I explained that my focus was on the children's work, she replied that she, too, had ideas to contribute. Certainly the dual roles of participant and observer can be frustrating, but moments of learning can grow from that tension. During reflection, first with the children, and then with the adults, the opportunities for drama growth multiply. When the community listens to its members revealing and commenting upon their experiences, everyone can benefit from the variety of observations being offered, selecting those reflections that will illuminate their own journeys. As well, children often write to me about our visits, and a new set of observations appears for further consideration. Teachers, too, bring back their thoughts in journals and papers, distanced from the moment, and placed in context within their own teaching lives, as evidenced by some of the insightful teacher comments included in this book.

Over the years, as teachers pondered my demonstrations, together in class and alone in their journals, I recognized that their collective reflections reveal all of the concerns we have in drama in education today. If we would listen to those educators working with children, and if we could become part of the negotiated meaning-making that grows from these interactions, then the teaching/learning process in drama could be revealed and clarified from within the truth of the classroom. The comments by the teachers in this book are drawn from their journals, their group interactions, and their post-course reflections. Their voices represent the variety of responses that emerged from teachers as they brought their own experiences to both participatory classroom demonstrations and seminars. Many teachers had worked with or read every drama authority in contemporary education; some of them were actors and storytellers, graduates of theatre arts programs; some were new to drama teaching but brought finely-honed curriculum-connected strengths.

My personal reflections here are interspersed with teacher comments that pertain to us as a teaching/learning community, and I have left them anonymous, because usually the thoughts of many have been caught by one voice. I have also transcribed the voices of the children, and I have included examples of their reflections and thoughts about drama experiences in letters that I have received from them, after they returned to their classrooms and their own school programs. These letters often reveal a moment in the drama I had missed or had misjudged, or demonstrate further insight by the children from the cool distance of "after the events." I treasure them, and each time I read through a bundle that a teacher has been kind enough to send along, I am struck again by the clarifying that occurs for all of us when we take time to consider the implications of the events in which we have participated.

*David Booth*
*Toronto, September 1994*

# 1

## *What Would You Rather Be?*
### (From Child Play into Drama)

We sometimes forget that children roleplay naturally from the time they can first move about: drama is the very stuff of their casual play — imagining an old crate a castle, a stool a horse, a paintbrush a magic wand.

John Burningham's picture book *Would You Rather. . .* shows how natural this play is, and provides a perfect vehicle for blending story and drama when working with children. It also provides a useful working model for an examination of the relationship between these two modes of learning. From the very first page, readers are inside the book, as the author invites them to make a choice from among three situations:

> Would you rather. . .
> Your house was surrounded by
> water, snow or jungle. . .

Immediately the children can begin choosing the environment that conjures up for them the most vivid images. When I add, "You are living in your house in that place at this very moment. Tell me what it is like," the element of dramatic involvement is introduced; the children spontaneously become a part of the literary fiction, identifying with their own particular vision of life "there and then" while working "here and now." Authors use this magic "as if" to draw the reader inside the life of a story, and drama works on the same premise. Children who have had experience in creating their own dramatized stories bring a greater sense of expectation to print, since the speculative nature of spontaneous roleplaying develops the ability to think creatively, to examine the many levels of meaning that underlie each action, and to develop the "what if" element that is necessary for reading. Just as a story can affect the drama to follow, the learning experience in drama can increase the child's storehouse of personal meanings, thus altering any meaning he or she brings to the text.

Because of the nature of my work, I generally meet a class of children once in a demonstration setting, and therefore I must choose books that draw an immediate response from the children, so that I can move them into a situation where we can begin building the "as if" world of drama. *Would You Rather* . . . opens doors at once with children of every grade level. As I read and show the book, I stop every so often to let the children contribute their responses and feelings about the author's ideas through storytelling and dramatic roleplaying. By questioning children as if they are in role, I can help them picture that world, and the role gives them the public voice with which to share the creations of their imaginations.

GRADE 1 CHILD: My house is surrounded by water.
DB: Do you live on an island, or perhaps a houseboat?
CHILD: A peninsula, but you can't get to the top end; it's land-locked by a mountain.
DB: Do you have a boat?
CHILD: Not a motor boat. No one in my family believes in them. We only use sailboats.
DB: Well, what do you do if there is an emergency and there is no wind?
CHILD: There is a kayak, and I can paddle it very fast and go for help. There is a boat ambulance on the mainland.

As I interact with the children, using their own ideas, I am able to help them to begin to understand the consequences of what they are seeing and saying, and together we fashion their own imaginings into a personal, coherent story. Dramatic roleplaying helps the children go one step beyond identifying and empathizing with the story; they begin to use the story elements to structure their own thoughts, reacting and responding personally, entering as deeply as they wish into the new world of meaning. Through drama, they may move from the particular experience of the story to a more general understanding of the nature of what is being explored, making explicit much of what is implied.

Would you rather be made to eat . . .
spider stew, slug dumplings, mashed worms,
or drink snail pop . . .

GRADE 5 CHILD: Snail pop.

DB: Where did you get it?

CHILD: Me and my dad make it every summer. First, you catch the snails. We invented these neat traps. Then you begin the process of turning them into the drink.

DB: How do you go about that?

CHILD: Well, it's all based on distillation. The important thing is that you just use the essence of snail, none of the meat.

DB: Why?

CHILD: It clogs the straws when you drink the pop.

DB: And what do you put the pop in?

CHILD: Cans.

DB: Why not bottles?

CHILD: Well, my dad and me used bottles once, but there was a problem. The night we did it, my dad woke me up at midnight, and he said that they were exploding all over the place because we had used too much yeast, and so we had to take all of the bottles into the backyard and bury them, so that no one would be hurt.

As this child built his personal story spontaneously in role by storytelling, he used his own knowledge and background to elaborate upon the literary stimulus. Drama tells me what a child has taken from a story, so that I can help him or her examine and explore the possibilities of what has been read, heard or viewed. Through such externalized representations as drama, children's perceptions are altered and expanded. As children grow in dramatic ability, they improve their communication skills — grappling with experiences, playing out problems and learning to use the conventions of the medium.

19

Would you rather ...
An elephant drank your bathwater
An eagle stole your dinner
A pig tried on your clothes
or a hippo slept in your bed?

These delightful choices can promote much lateral thinking among the children, as they hitchhike on each other's stories — elaborating, extending and inventing scenarios that help them make sense of the ridiculous, building networks of meaning from each imaginative situation.

GRADE 1 CHILD: An elephant stole my bathwater.
DB: Were you in the bath at the time?
CHILD: Yes.
DB: Do you mean the elephant drank the dirty bathwater?
CHILD: No! Elephants just put the water up their trunk so that they can use it later on.
DB: Was the elephant a pet, was it from the circus or was it a wild one?
CHILD: It was the neighbor's.

GRADE 4 CHILD: An eagle stole my dinner.
DB: What were you having for dinner?
CHILD: Every vegetable you can think of.

DB: A pig tried on your clothes?
GRADE 2 CHILD: Yes, my jeans, my T-shirt, my socks and my Adidas.
DB: Why do you think it did that?
CHILD: It wanted to see me naked.

DB: A hippo slept in your bed? Did it break it?
GRADE 1 CHILD: Yes, but it didn't mean to.
DB: What did your mother say?
CHILD: Well, I was afraid to tell the truth, because I had been warned about having all of these zoo creatures in my room, and my parents had just bought me this new bed that had been smashed to bits.
DB: So what did you say to them?
CHILD: I told the truth, because I knew that somehow they would understand.
DB: You must have very fine parents.
CHILD: They're great.

When children read a story, it is the dynamic of narrative that propels them forward. Often in school we stress the ability to analyse after the story, rather than the skills of making meaning happen during the interactive mode of reading. Of course, teachers who are assisting children to learn to read will have to develop strategies that help the children work inside the print mode, as they experience the words. Drama can nurture this ability.

> Would your rather...
> Your dad did a dance at school
> or your mom had a fight in a café?

These two pictures usually take the child on a different journey. In drama, there is the *self* that one begins with, and the *other* that one takes on. At times, the *self* is the motive force of the drama, dictating words and action from personal background and from a particular value system; at other times, the *adopted persona* is dominant, presenting a complex subject to explore through talk and drama. *Role* is the juxtaposition of these two parts, so that the learning is viewed internally but from a new or different perspective. (It is interesting to note that the illustrations in *Would You Rather...* feature the same child character in each scene, as if the same *self* were involved in each new situation.)

In working with these choices concerning parents, I found that the responses were filtered through the personal experiences of the children. Those who imagined their dads doing a dance at school had interesting reasons — he did it to raise money for the Home and School Association, cheer up a class that had done poorly on a test, or take part in an ethnic festival's activities. No one was embarrassed; everyone seemed to think that it would be a positive experience for both the dad and the class. However, when they depicted in small groups a mother's fight in a restaurant, there were many conflicting emotions, most of them centring on the mother. Many children in their reconstructions defended the mother's actions, but all were embarrassed.

GRADE 5 CHILD: We were in the McDonald's restaurant. My mother was in line, when suddenly a man butted in front of her. Right away, my mother's lover came up and told that guy to get back into line...

Story after story concerned wrongs being righted, emotions overruling reason, families in disagreement. The scene triggered the playing out of many stored-up tensions. The *self* and the *other* were melding, and the children found themselves united in their feelings about the arguments. This intersection of the children's private worlds and the world of the story produces power for building comprehension and response. A resonant relationship is set up between the individual responses of the students and the story. The children begin interacting with the story in ever-widening ways, adding to their childhood gardens an awareness of the lives of other classmates, the world of the author and their new-found perceptions in role. (Burningham's Everychild is shown to be embarrassed in each situation.)

In a regular class with time to develop the situations, each of the ideas can be the beginning of a full-fledged drama lesson as well as a stimulus for word play and dramatic brainstorming.

> Would you rather be lost...
> In the fog, at sea,
> in a desert,
> in a forest
> or in a crowd...

Each of these settings has been the basis for building a whole-class drama lesson. The dramas have varied widely with the interests of the group. We have discovered missing cities arising from the mists of the past; we have been in lifeboats lost on the sea and have found an island from *Lord of the Flies*; we have searched for water in a desert, only to find it was controlled by an evil king; we have found in the forest a society of people who have lived underground for their entire lives; we have been lost in a crowd of aliens, unable to reveal our true identities until we could find someone we knew to be trustworthy.

Children learn to read through personal relationships with parents, teachers and others who can read, and the process of reading becomes an extension of these relationships. Children relate to story in terms of their own identities, just as they do to their families, friends and environments. Their stories have to fit with their own experiences and with the expectations of their communities. By responding to other people's cues and by receiving responses from them, children further establish their own identities, borrowing from others to see how their stories fit together. Children explore life through their own stories and those of others, creating their own unique narratives and ways of representing yesterday, today and tomorrow.

Would you rather...
Your house was surrounded by water,
snow
or jungle

A Grade 1 class had chosen their environments. Each child was demonstrating the difficulties and pleasures of his or her particular setting, and I was observing them and gently prodding them with specific questions about the nature of their lifestyles. A child with Down's Syndrome was making angels in the snow, and, unsure of his abilities, I began asking him questions.

DB: Is your house surrounded by snow?
(Child nods affirmatively.)
DB: Do you like living here in the snow?
(Child again nods yes.)
DB: Are you the King of Winter?
(Child nods yes.)
DB: Then what are you wearing on your head?
CHILD: A crown of ice.

I want children to wear crowns of ice in summer, have eagles steal their vegetables, let hippos sleep in their beds, take breakfast in balloons, and get lost in childhood gardens. As also, I am certain, would John Burningham.

REAL PLAY, REAL PRETENDING

As if there were a basic difference between the fairy tale that a child made up himself and one that was created for him by imaginative folk or by a good writer!... It makes no difference whether or not the child is offered fairy tales for, if he is not, he becomes his own Andersen, Grimm, Ershov. Moreover, all his playing is a dramatization of a fairy tale which he creates on the spot, animating, according to his fancy, all objects — converting any stool into a train, into a house, into an airplane, or into a camel.

Korneii Chukofsky, *From Two to Five*

Play is vital to the development of children. We watch as they grow and learn spontaneously in their play time — talking, developing their imaginations, ordering and making sense of their experiences through their own observations and impressions. Many kindergarten and grade one classrooms have facilities that encourage dramatic play, ranging from a "drama centre" to a well-equipped room or area. Materials such as boxes, cloaks, hats, tools and models can often stimulate undirected play. Some teachers assign groups to certain areas, such as a cooking centre, in order to encourage roleplaying; others may allow dramatic play as a response to a story, a discussion or a particular theme.

The transition from children's dramatic play to more adventurous drama must be approached carefully. When my four-year-old son roleplayed the story of *Snow White* with me over a period of months, he reminded me at all times to "stick to the story," not to elaborate or extend the details, and to work within his predetermined ritualistic confines. Only when he entered kindergarten did he begin to allow "what if..." to creep into the play. When, as the witch, he asked me as Snow White if I wanted an apple, I could at last reply, "No thanks, but I would enjoy a juicy ripe pear," and he in turn could say, "I just happen to have a pear right here in my basket. Try biting the bright yellow inside!" He had moved from straight replaying of the story into improvisational drama, entering a frame with no particular ending and no plotline to fixate upon. It was a new Snow White, and he and I were engaged in versioning, in creating our own fairy tale within a structured drama context.

A few years ago a friend of mine from England, David Davis, was visiting me with his five-year-old daughter, Elaine. I was captivated by her ability to roleplay with him as they recreated *Little Red Riding Hood*. I managed to find, at her request, a basket and a tea towel to hide the goodies. It was with obvious delight that she took part in the familiar and yet always new dramatization, and her father was able to present a wonderfully vile wolf. When it was suggested that I portray the wolf in play with the child, I took the chance, and the dramatic play began as before. I followed her lead, maintaining the story. The work progressed until I said, "The better to see you with." At this moment, Elaine turned to her father and said that she didn't want to play anymore. The dramatic play had disappeared with the sudden reality of the situation: there was no story for protection and projection, only a real wolf in a real kitchen. Elaine had taught me that drama must be fictional, a medium for learning that uses art as a means of symbolizing reality and helping us to understand that reality.

As teachers, we can facilitate the dramatic play environment, helping children expand their themes and extending and supplementing the language and the play with appropriate attitudes, approaches and strategies. We can guide the action, encourage particular activity, question the children about what is happening and even enter the play situation by taking on a role ourselves. Observation of their play can help us plan lessons based on their experiences when it is time to introduce them to directed activities in drama. We can find, in undirected activities, new directions for more formal drama lessons which will help children experiment, consider alternatives, work in groups and order their ideas. As Richard Courtney points out, much dramatic play takes place outside the control of the teacher. However, careful structure and intervention can support and guide the children's work without diminishing their own creative direction or ideas.

When my son was five, he used to talk to himself in play, and I was struck by the importance of play exploration in language development. Through projected play in which he manipulated and gave voice to toy symbols and through dramatic play in which he himself was inside the medium of drama, he used words and registers unavailable to him for a variety of reasons in non-play situations. Every aspect of language was investigated: he played multiple roles, changing at rapid-fire speed, adapting his voice qualities to the demands of the particular character and altering syntax to fit the situation. He was inside the play looking at his own creations as spectator, and refocusing and elaborating where and when necessary. There can be no doubt that dramatic play is vital to language growth. The question is, can we continue this languaging mode through educational drama, in which roleplay and improvisation are used as a medium for learning?

Dramatic play takes place in an imaginative frame that depends upon language for its existence. The talk in play shapes and develops themes, encourages cohesion and provides opportunities for meeting individual needs. The interactive feedback by the participants helps them bring together experience and create knowledge, as they plan, discuss, support, reject and clarify. The feeling and the challenge of playing roles give the players new ways to gain experience, perception and insight, and enriched language skill is not just a byproduct: it grows from the play, because of the play, and structures the play, all at once.

## WHERE WILL THE CHILDREN PLAY?

I was working with a group of teachers in a summer program where we were to engage a kindergarten class in a structured drama experience, and analyse the teaching techniques that were used as the work progressed. Four teachers began the work, involving thirty children in creating a play park. The children sang camp songs, told of favorite park activities and then began to mime the use of play equipment in small groups, locating the park in time and space within the classroom. Each group described or demonstrated its playground creations to other groups.

As this was happening, another teacher in role — wearing a safety helmet — was posting signs around the room that read, "Playground to be closed and replaced with a building." Eventually, the children began to notice the signs, and those who could read told the others about the impending development. The children began to stop their park play. They complained vehemently to the teacher in role as park supervisor that their park should not be destroyed for a building. I focused the discussion around what could be done and the children made posters of protest, which they later mounted over the signs. They also composed a collective letter of complaint to the mayor. Then the lesson stopped for the day.

At the next session, the children began by singing their camp songs, followed by a brief discussion reviewing the previous lesson's proceedings. The class was divided into four small groups with one teacher/leader per group, to air and solidify the children's objections to the building. The whole class gathered to confront one teacher in role as a city planner, who explained that a home for senior citizens was to be built on the park land. The children presented their arguments, and the planner was sympathetic, but she firmly stated the project was going ahead.

A teacher re-entered in the role of Mrs. Marshall, an older woman who wanted to move into the new building. As the children questioned her, they began to examine the necessity for the building on the park land. The teacher in role refocused the energies of the class toward alternatives to the confrontation, using ideas from the children to "build" a drama. Mrs. Marshall revealed that the home she was leaving had a very large lot attached to it, and she would be willing to donate this lot to the city as a playground. The children accepted this as a satisfactory solution. They re-established the playground in the new area through action and words, with the teachers in role as playground supervisors. In a sense, they ended where they had begun.

Two aspects of these lessons stand out as particularly significant: the change in the direction of the drama when the children recognized the signs' implications for their fictional playground, and the shift in tension and feeling when they understood Mrs. Marshall's need for a new home. They had moved through dramatic play to group consensus in a reflective mode. They were not just demanding their own rewards but considering and comprehending the needs of others.

This type of emotional/cognitive experiencing, followed by reflective distancing, is the hallmark of drama. In this kind of work, the play roots of the drama lesson are clearly in evidence. The children were very close to being themselves, working with familiar situations and attitudes. Then they gradually adopted roles as determined by the situation. When the children who read the sign said, "They're going to get rid of the park," the roleplaying and the drama began.

## PLAYING INSIDE THE DRAMA

Elliott Eisner, in *The Mythology of Art Education*, writes that it is a myth that children need only materials, motivation and encouragement in order to develop in the arts: "The ability to use [an artform] as a vehicle for expression is in large measure a learned ability and the teacher has a much more complex task than simply providing materials and encouragement."

There will, of course, be times when children will engage in drama in a spontaneous and open-ended structure, maintaining the "as if" situation and developing the action without intervention by the teacher. They will be working in a play mode, and may resent being moved into a more structured way of learning with a focus that attempts to unite the whole group. They may need time to work this way for a while, continuing to build physical belief in the drama situation, concretizing the details and the environment. However, children may also require structures that enable the feelings and responses they have to be explored, clarified, modified and transformed into something that can be understood and reflected upon.

My job is to help the children find a drama focus acceptable to the majority of the class, not to direct the drama or just have the children follow orders. I try not to provide answers, but instead manage the situation — applying pressure and deepening the experience where necessary. It is a continual process of organization and reorganization, of focusing and refocusing. I must try to see the implications of every suggestion and then find an appropriate strategy for utilizing the ideas for the larger, overall education goals of the group.

A teacher enrolled in a specialist drama course asked how she might improve her puppet work with junior students. Her working methods were simple: she bought quantities of materials for the puppet-making, initiated the activity in groups of five and assisted where necessary. She felt that the resulting puppet plays showed little originality, and no depth of emotion or experience. And yet, the teacher hesitated to alter the direction of the work, afraid to intervene in the flow of the children's ideas.

As a drama consultant, I wandered through all the grades in many different schools and was shocked to discover that in some secondary theatre arts classes television commercials seemed to be the single source of "improvs." The teacher paid homage to pedagogy by questioning the class about each skit at its end, generally hoping for some astute theatrical criticism, but ending up often with students personally attacking each other's work.

A drama teacher once explained to me his method of teaching drama: he motivated the class with a suitable source or activity, divided them into groups, dictated the exercise and then left the room for thirty-five minutes while the students worked. He would return for the last ten minutes when the groups would share their presentations. His idea was to free the imagination of the children through free expression. And, of course, he found that the drama was of little significance.

While teachers must care about self-expression, we must also be deeply concerned about development — cognitive and affective — in a social context, and we must not be averse to or afraid of setting up structures that assist children in working in the experiential medium of drama, helping them to gain control over it, and to find new insights and understanding.

Some children can't believe in "the big lie," can't accept the magic "what if." They seem locked into their present reality; an imagined world is outside their ken. What are the blocks to their suspending disbelief, and how does this inability affect so much of what these children think about in all aspects of their lives? Is letting go of the "here and now" such a painful release? What do they feel they are hanging on to — image, self, past — and when they do take flight on drama wings, can they remain airborne?

Tony was ten years old and couldn't find the sand in the desert — he only saw linoleum on the studio floor. "There ain't no sand! There ain't no desert!" There ain't no drama. No matter the framework of the lesson, Tony never left the actual space of the room. Gradually the class ignored his constant complaints of non-belief, and their drama work progressed. They created a robot world where humans weren't valued, and Tony hung about on the fringe of the action, never participating, but trying not to disturb — a wallpaper student. On parents' night, I usually demonstrated with the children as their parents watched, recreating a piece of work they had explored, and using theatre crafts (lighting, masks, etc.) to heighten the experience for participants and spectators. In a moment of darkness, Tony, who had in his generosity been going through the motions, turned to me and said, "Is that my mother sitting there?"

"Yes, Tony."

"Is this a play we're doing?"

"Yes, Tony."

"Oh."

He was inside the moment of unlived life as quickly as if he had stepped through a mirror. Why had I failed to reach him until then?

Some children simply tag along until suddenly the situation, the tension or the group pulls them inside the drama, and they begin to think "as if." Perhaps others need more formal approaches for allowing themselves to enter the imaginary garden. I wonder if they played as preschool infants, if they saw only a sandbox and not a city, sat inside a cardboard carton and not a space capsule, baked playdough circles and not pies. Or is it a rejection of play roles, a deliberate refusal to step back and look at life in a new way? How much trust in self does it take to creep into others' shoes, if only for thirty minutes while standing on linoleum in a faraway desert?

I have watched some adults — teachers — fight the big lie. Even though they know they are working in an artform that requires active participation, they hold back, either acting in a stereotyped manner or sabotaging the drama, unable to be part of the creative activity that is co-operative and celebratory, living through a fictional yet completely real experience. Often they tell me that nothing was happening, and so they decided to instigate a new drama direction, rather than listening to and observing their fellow participants and letting the power of the art build the framework. It is sometimes very difficult to let oneself fall into the collective creation voluntarily. Drama is perhaps the only art dependent on no one person and everyone all at once.

Because drama is a social process, the children should be concerned with the ideas of others, with fitting their own thoughts and feelings into the group effort. They will be negotiating for both shared and personal meanings through their interactions, both in and out of role, developing an awareness of form and control from inside the drama. But as in their sandbox deserts, pretending must be "real."

# 2

## Entering the Story Cave
### (Connecting Story and Drama)

STORY AS A THOUSAND-FACED CREATION

Many of the stories and songs are as old as the hills, and possess
some of the same earth-browned warmth and wonder that nature
cherishes: others were minted today and stink of gasoline fumes
and pulsate with the rhythm of engines. But all of these bits of
language have a commodity they share: they are the voice of men
telling us about themselves — the dreams, the wars, the yearn-
ing for love, the tricks and sly pranks, the banquets and crusts,
the prayers for peace, the rape of mountain and river and the
thousand-faced creation that each of us is.

Ramon Ross, *Storyteller*

Story is a basic way of organizing our human experiences, a
framework for learning. We search for our own stories in the
stories of others. Story — narrative — is never simply plot. "Story
is a primary act of mind," writes Barbara Hardy in *The Cool Web*.
"Narrative, like lyric or dance, is not to be regarded as an aesthetic invention used by artists to control, manipulate and order
experiences, but as this primary act of mind transferred to art
from life." What concerns Hardy are the qualities that fictional
narrative shares with the inner and outer storytelling that play
a major role in the child's sleeping and waking life. She says
that storying is our constant attempt at exchanging identities and
remaking the past, a mode of looking back in order to go forward.
Storying is such an active process. We make stories, live them,

remember or forget them, tell them, reshape them, pass them on, write them down, sing, act and paint them. Children speak almost entirely through stories — real or invented — and they comprehend what others say through story.

I visited a grade two class in an inner-city school, surrounded by lead smelters and all types of pollution. The principal had requested my help in bringing a drama program to the children to give them images other than the view from the school's grimy windows. I don't know why I chose an Old Testament story. Perhaps the book was near my desk and caught my eye. Or did I need extra strength to walk through those doors into a fogged-in school? Clyde Robert Bulla's illustrations of Joseph and his family are dark and full of mystery, and they challenged my own understanding of the story. I wanted these children to work as one, and I created Jacob and his "thirty-two children" as a setting for the drama, in a time and place far from their city.

We built a desert community, and they chose sheep and goats to herd. We found an oasis, cleared the sand, built troughs for water for the animals and passed around a basket of dates to taste (real fruit that added a reality base to the drama). We then had a visit from Jacob (myself in role) and a child in role as his favorite son:

"My sons," I said, "you have worked well. Tomorrow Joseph here will return with fresh fruit and wine to cool you in this heat. It is almost time to return to the settlement for the fall season. I look forward to having my sons around me again. And do you like Joseph's new coat? I made it myself. Strange how my skills as a tent-maker have come in so handy. I bid you farewell."

We sat in a circle, and they told stories of their work and the heat and the soft life of Joseph; their anger grew and they plotted to get rid of him. I had not read them the story, but they drew from memories of it and from folklore and decided to sell him to traders. This was accomplished through mime with me in role as an Egyptian trader. Then it was time to go home to Jacob.

DB: I am so happy my sons are back. Is Joseph arriving later?
1st CHILD: Joseph isn't coming.
DB: Has he been detained?
2nd CHILD: He can't come.
DB: Why not?
1st CHILD: He's dead.

DB: What do you mean, he's dead?
1st CHILD: He was killed.
DB: How was he killed?
1st CHILD: By a sheep.
DB: And how did a sheep kill him?
3rd CHILD: It smothered him to death.
DB: My son, smothered to death by a sheep.

*(And no one laughed or spoke. The children felt my grief.)*

The first boy brought meaning to the fictional situation, using the context we had built, the milieu of shepherds in the desert. He couldn't think of any dangers to Joseph other than sheep, and the second child supported him: to maintain the drama, he decided on the spot that the essence of sheep was wool and all wool could do was smother. By believing in their belief rather than questioning it, I could continue the drama.

The honesty of these children's struggle is the quality of education that I am after. Give me sheep as killers any day instead of surface, glib answers provided for the amusement of all. I am impressed with the struggle, with the journey. Thirty-two children in my tent, and we understood Jacob, Joseph and the brothers.

Later in the day, I watched the children in the playground. Their small bodies seemed as grey as the tarmac, but they ran with urchin energy, and as their words filtered up to my classroom window, I realized they were chasing one boy and shouting, "Get Joseph! Get Joseph!" Oh, that coat of many colors.

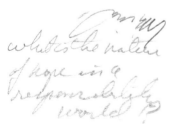

RAILROAD, DIGGING IN THE MINE

...ed fruit in the Chinese orchards near
...rs would gather in the shack after a hot,
...e of the ways that the old-timers would
...eep came was to tell stories.

...far from escapist maneuvers. What Kenneth Burke said of proverbs is equally true of folktales: They are strategies for living. At the very least, the stories offered consolation and more often hope. But beyond that, the stories also expressed the loneliness, anger, fear, and love that were part of the Chinese-American experience.

Lawrence Yep,
*The Rainbow People*

33

In his book *Tales from Gold Mountain*, Paul Yee has achieved a remarkable goal, the blending of Chinese folktales with the historical incidents of the immigration to Canada of Chinese men to work on the building of the national railway and in the gold rush of the north. These stories hold the spirits of children in the strangest of ways. I want to explore each one in drama and to try to discover the secrets Paul Yee has buried in his tellings. Certainly the weaving of folklore and historical incidents offers us as teachers dozens of universal truths that can be tapped into for dramatic exploration.

One grade eight class listened to me tell the tale of *Rider Chan*, in which a young man carries messages, gold and medicine to the workers in the fields during the Gold Rush. As he crosses a river, his leg is grabbed by a ghost, and released only when Chan agrees to bury the corpses of dead workers lost in the river, so that they may have eternal rest. The situation of the ghosts in the river represents the very stuff of drama — children can rise from the floor, moving ghoul-like towards the rider on shore, entreating the living one to help them. The drama offers the opportunity to explore the duality of roles: the ghosts negotiating with the living, and the children attempting to convince Chan, in this case me, the teacher, working in role. The students were excellent at argument, logical thinkers used to debate and to winning. I wanted to touch upon the heart of the drama, the emotional power of the situation, the aesthetic quality of characters felt and understood through being in role. As the children formed small groups in role as ghosts, to plan strategies for convincing Chan to symbolically bury them and then return their dust to China, their ideas gradually turned towards a son's devotion to his mother and to the respect his culture demonstrated towards the memory of loved ones lost. When, as a class, they then positioned themselves as if in the river, speaking to the living on shore, their words evidenced a passionate attempt to move the heart of Chan. They regrouped several times to draw up new arguments, new ways of reaching Chan. It was not until they themselves felt the frustration and the need to change Chan's mind that the drama began to happen. They were no longer merely students play-acting in a classroom — they were in a river struggling to get out. Their language altered; they chose their words carefully, adding the weight of feeling; they used their arms, their bodies to supplement their cries of anguish; they had become a more compact group physically, taking strength from each other by standing shoulder to shoulder; they were coming to grips with the power of theatre, knowing how to effect change in others through their roles, using voice and stance and presence in order to persuade. And when I agreed to the plan of ritual burial, they felt satisfaction both inside the drama as the ghosts in pain, and outside the drama as students who had met the artistic and moral challenge presented by a teacher.

Later, when I had read two other selections from this book of tales to the class, the questions about the time period grew along with suggestions for new drama work, generated by the story and by the children's concerns about the Chinese workers. This lesson, then, could serve as the beginning for extended playmaking, depicting life in North America for Chinese workers.

Several children even sent me poems reflecting upon their story work that day, showing how they had expanded their understanding of the original story through their dramatization of it. The following is one of the poems.

*Remember*

Remember all my thoughts, my words
For I am gone now, like a bird.
My body rests underground, but
My spirit ventures somewhere sound.
Everything I did and said
Recalled upon my own deathbed.
Just for now I want to say,
"Look at me where I lay."
In my eyes do you see
Anything resembling me?
Now I leave you with no word
For I am gone now, like a bird.

Melanie

As a teacher, I yearned for more time to explore other extensions of the drama, but it was clear that the children were already on their way to making the story their own. More and more, I find it is the children who determine the lesson, revealing to me which points are significant and which characters should come to the forefront, so that they can own the work. I construct the lesson, but they create the drama.

In the following case, the connection between the play of the young child and the drama experience of school children was evident from the first moment the children entered the room. The class was composed of twenty-five boys, aged five and six years, attending a summer camp within a school setting. I had chosen another tale by Paul Yee, but rather than read aloud "Spirits of the Railway," I had asked a group of teachers on course the day before to prepare to tell the tale as an ensemble, weaving the story around the children, and making use of a parachute to draw everyone physically inside the story circle. After listening to the story, the boys retold it to me as we sat together in a large bay window area. One teacher later wrote:

> David did not read the story. Instead, the adults in the class became group storytellers, sharing the story in role, and using a parachute to gather the children around. The parachute was a powerful symbol. Amazingly enough, the boys retained all of the information from the storytelling. This came as a surprise to me.
>
> The joy of the story and its telling! So spontaneous, so supportive of teacher for teacher and teacher for child. The children clutching the parachute, just the joy of pulling the parachute up and down delighted the children as it became a mountain, or waves, or a covering. It *felt* good. It gave us all something to cling to in tentative beginnings and something to soar with as we sailed through the story. I loved the storytelling and when in discussion found the use of the parachute to be spontaneous and delighted in it even more. The work happened and was allowed to happen through careful planning and then letting go. We should all "let go" and enjoy the parachutes more!

In role as railway workers, the children sat in a large circle, preparing to leave for the new world. We passed around chunks of bread, as a symbol of our memories of home life, and I narrated some of the problems ahead of us. Each child said goodbye to their families.

> The bread was significant. Almost eating part of this imaginary world. Bread — a bonding agent. I was afraid the bread would distract them but it didn't. The beauty of the bread was that it wasn't Oreo cookies. What is more communal than breaking

bread? So valuable a bonding experience.

There was this magnificent moment that helped me to understand the beauty of this method of teaching/creating dramas. Ben, my son in the drama, was packing to go to the new world. We finished packing and words were welling up inside of him and he was looking directly into my eyes. I waited for him to speak and he didn't at first. Gently, I asked him if he had something to say and he pulled these words up from his soul and simply said, "I'm going." He delivered those two words so meaningfully and powerfully. He seemed to understand the significance of this decision to leave his mother and go to a strange land. I will never forget that moment.

TLR    In role as the captain, I called for volunteers to sign up for the long voyage from China to North America, offering jobs, shoes and gold nuggets to all those who were accepted for the journey. The boys actually signed their names on the ship's registry, and the story drama began.

> At one point, early in the session, the boys were lined up in front of David who was in role as the ship captain. They broke out into a chant of "I'm looking at you!" [apparently a familiar camp song]. David just let this run its course — a clear example of play — then on to adding tension to deepen their belief in the drama: "Sign up and get your gold nugget!" David announced. The very process of signing their names on the yellow pad of paper by each of the children in role deepened their work.
>
> I really liked David's question: "Is anyone in this group strong enough to remember the message of his father's ghost?" Almost all of the boys raised their hands, and this was a prelude of the drama work to come. The challenge was to get this group of boys to believe in the drama, to "be" serious mine workers, or, in other words, to move from play to dramatic play to drama.

Using a scene from the story concerning workers who would not enter a mine because of ghost voices, I set up the situation where the children as miners would persuade the teachers as reluctant workers to enter the tunnel. This was followed by the next scene, where as the boys in role slept in their bunks, the teachers as spirits whispered words of advice to them concerning the dangers of entering the mine.

As a class, the children shared their stories from the night visitors together, and the drama grew from the need to give all of

37

the bodies of those killed in the mine disaster a decent burial. I asked the teachers to lie quietly on the floor while all the children gently covered them with the parachute.

> For these boys the aesthetic moment (and what a moment it was!) came at the end of the drama when they symbolically buried the adults with the parachute. They believed in what they were doing.

The work ended as the children bowed three times to the mine leader, and the story drama was complete.

These children seemed too young for such extended, focused drama, and I attempted to bring into the lesson as much dramatic play as I could. I was thankful for the parachute, the bread and the teachers who followed my lead like the most sensitive of ensemble players, foregoing their own directorial urges, and helping me to find within those pure childhood hearts the fragile moments of collective playmaking. I shall never forget the burial. The children should not have been able to do that, but they did. They gave us more than we deserved.

> Little boys so small that I almost stepped on one. (But that is fair because one almost stepped on me during the end of the drama. I would not have minded at that point.) Little boys with grins and glints of devilment and wiggles and joy. Little boys that are the same age as my daughter. She, for the moment, seems like the only shred of a connection I seem to have with them, and they are boys. I think of them, after the fact, and realize they have helped me see her in a new light, and I see them through the vision of Aurelia. As I think of her, it begins to dawn on me what they are ... the instant of being brilliant beyond years, on the edge of tears, lunging forward into laughter at the turn of a thought, the depths, the strangely wonderful and unique humor, the single-mindedness and determination to stick to their guns, right or wrong, mixed with a deep desire to please me for the sake of pleasing me ... the sheer delight of being six. I realize tonight that I have missed being totally delighted in them and I am very sad. I have looked at them but not really seen them, save for a few minutes. I have been very self-centred, which has made for a less satisfying lesson for myself and for the children. I have become so used to the junior high mind, body and spirit, that I have missed a chance to see from where this spirit evolves. I realize that I am not totally focused on them, neither am I involved

enough in the moment. This realization is helpful because it clears the path for tomorrow's work. My mission, simply to be there, fully there with the children, the children who are actually there. Not the ones I wish to be there, but the ones who are there.

LEARNING TO STORY

How can drama assist children in building their own stories? How can we become co-constructors of the story with the children? There is "The Story" and there is "The Story of the Drama."

> Storying is the process of narrative-telling. In trying to find "essential meanings in life," we objectify our experiences by translating them into narrative, which we may then play out in our mind and which we may also communicate to others. Even when an experience is intensely personal, turning it into a story allows us to explore it, to organize it, to reflect upon it, and to communicate it. All this is our attempt to find our own private meanings in the experience. Storying provides students with a natural human process for finding "essential meanings" in the life-experiences of themselves and others. Its role in language learning is critical, for it provides opportunities for students to search for and discover these "essential meanings in life". This is what education is all about.
>
> Bill Manson

Drama allows us to tell stories, to engage in the art of narrative. The simplest retelling of yesterday's events is an act of imagination, as we have the option of reinventing the characters, experiences, circumstances, motivations and outcomes. Fictional storytelling, like drama, encompasses and extends the possibilities of human experience. Perhaps higher-level thought could be called "brain fiction," built up by the narrative mind, as Harold Rosen put it. Drama may be one of the few language situations that opens up story possibilities, that allows spontaneous narrative to enter naturally into the flow of talk — every kind of story from personal experience to literary fictions — so that the narrative mode can be an integral part of the school curriculum.

Rosen says that "stories-in-the-head" should be given their chance to be heard. In making meaning from the stories of others, children must go back and forth between the story they are reading or listening to, and the stories they know — their own personal narratives. They are in a very real sense building a personal story from the other fiction alongside their own experiences, attempting to make sense of the story in order to make meaning in their lives. Until the child can make his or her story from the fictional one, there is no story for that child. The process of story continues beyond the end as the seed of another story readies itself for germination. Fred Inglis calls culture "the collection of stories we tell to ourselves about ourselves."

Drama is the act of crossing into the world of story. In sharing drama, we agree to live as if the story we are enacting were true. We imagine the story, engage with it, struggle with its unfamiliar concepts, associate our own experience with it and fill in its shape with our particular interpretation. We process the key events, images and themes of story by living them out in drama. The process holds true whether the stimulus for the drama is a written story, an oral tale or a group narration. Drama enables us to discover the heart of story through its images. The voice of the group resonates off the voice of the text to create the voice of the drama.

Using the ideas of a story as cues for their own dramatic responses allows children to test the implications of what is written and of their own responses to it. As teacher, I can draw upon the vast resources of the story as a way of stimulating and enriching the children's search for meaning in drama. Groups can test and clarify the implications of the text collectively, so that each person can see the difference in the various perceptions and interpretations, and can then make decisions about his or her own responses.

In teaching children to read, we need to develop structures to help them work inside the print mode, as they experience the words. Similarly, teachers who are working with children in drama need to find ways of promoting learning as the drama is happening, not just afterwards, in presentation or in reflection time.

In drama and in narrative, the context may be fictional but the emotional responses are real. Although the child is in a make-believe situation in story and in drama, the real world continues to exist, and the learning for the child lies in the negotiation of meanings — symbolic and literal — taking place in both spheres.

Drama helps children wander in the story garden, reconstructing symbols, images and narrative sequences through action. They re-examine the story's ideas, experimenting with them, learning to "play" with the narrative and then, in reflection, coming to an understanding of both the story's possibilities and the artform used to create it.

Drama can help children see beyond literal meaning, even subconsciously, so that an understanding of the complexity and subtlety of meaning is applied to the story. The children pause in a fictional present, linger on an image, move forward, backwards and sideways, in an attempt to make meaning happen. Time can be altered, ideas juxtaposed. If story is being used as the source of a drama, then the child brings to the text an ability to hypothesize, to identify with and clarify what is happening in the story, in the drama and in his or her own life. The learning is integrated as he or she engages with the two artforms. When the child has translated a written symbol into experience, he or she can then re-examine the story in the light of this new experience. Drama lets us take a journey, as Tolkien says, "there and back again."

I found Caldwell Cook's *The Play Way* (1917) an amazing record of a teacher's work with story and drama. It was the earliest book written proposing the use of drama in this way. Before that, drama in schools was usually concerned with the production of the school play. Cook believed that children learn better from doing and experiencing than from just reading and listening.

Beginning in 1920 in the United States, Winnifrid Ward, working at Northwestern University, developed her theory of story dramatization, in which a group of children make a story come alive by playing it out informally, without elaborate scripts or sets. Some drama authorities attacked the limitations of story dramatization, claiming that the goals of enactment are unclear; that the students may imitate dramatic moments rather than actually experience them; that the desire to get the sequence of events from the story in the right order may lessen the understanding of the greater meanings in the story; that improvisational work may descend to repeating trivial details in an attempt to recreate the right "facts" from the story. These are important concerns for the teacher of drama but they may be a result not of using a story as a stimulus for drama, but rather of not understanding what the value of the story is in its relationship to drama.

41

Making sense of a story demands that the children apply their own experiences to those in the story. The teacher must constantly help the children go back and forth between the story and their own responses to it, translating the experiences of the story into the context of their own lives. Drama, then, allows the children's own subjective world to come into play, helping them understand the meanings of the story as they live through the drama experience. If narrative and drama give form to thought and feeling, can we make use of one to build the other? Are they two sides of one coin? Do I risk diminishing one if I include the other at the same time in my teaching? Can we use drama to clarify and strengthen the reading of story, and can we use the story to stimulate or enlighten the drama work? Is it possible for the children to be engaged in learning both through drama and through reading in the same frame of reference? How do we engage children in the life blood of the story?

When children read or listen to a story, they are creating personal images in their minds. In drama, they are helping to build group images. How will they go about these tasks? Will they improvise within the story, stand on the story's shoulders or build on the story by designing new contexts or by finding analogies and patterns? How will they place it alongside others, building a set of stories for future reference?

Instead of planning in a vacuum, I can begin with a story that I know well, and find the power of drama within it. I can draw on the resources of the story — its situations, characters, problems, relationships, mood, atmosphere, texture and, especially, its concepts — as a way of stimulating and enriching the children's exploration in drama. Both story and drama demonstrate a concern for people — their values, their beliefs, the experiences they live through.

Educator Gavin Bolton says that the teacher must consider the story from its broadest themes before planning the drama; all questions must prod the children's thinking toward the development of universal themes and concepts. The teacher must search for a possible starting point that is relevant to the children's experience and relevant to the spirit of the story.

Replaying the story through a literal enactment of the plot may have occasional value, but the teacher should not feel limited to it. Furthermore, the response in these sorts of enactments may be limited to one of memory or recapitulation.

Story drama frees the teacher and children from the pressure of acting out the whole story or remembering a script. Most important, the children are allowed to bring what they know to the drama: the drama then engages their imaginations, and they inevitably move closer to the story. In this sense, the drama may even explore the story at one remove through an analogy that unlocks internal comprehension. Because of the brain's ability to use metaphor, it can use the pattern of one set of images to organize quite a different set. Therefore, the images from one story can be used as images for related and yet different meanings. Story drama opens the door to an endless number of linkages in the curriculum.

# 3

## *Paper Bag Faces*
### (Planning for Drama)

OLIVER HYDE HAS MOVED TO DETROIT

There was an album, Will the Circle Be Unbroken, that I was listening to a lot, and although I cannot make music, I wanted to honor it, especially the fiddle. There is also an old Irish tune about a man who fiddled on his way to the gallows and broke his fiddle across his knee before ascending to be hanged, so that "none other shall play on thee." He had murdered his faithless lover, I believe.

Richard Kennedy

I was teaching a course outside Detroit to sixty elementary teachers who were taking credits toward their graduate degrees, a language arts course with drama as a focus. The subject was new to the teachers, and they approached participating in role with some trepidation. I structured the two-week course around games and activities that allowed for co-operative experiencing in role, and the group developed a gentle awareness of improvisation and of how role is based on self and situation, but I wanted to move them into a story drama that might draw them more deeply into the complexities of role. I chose the picture book *Oliver Hyde's Dishcloth Concert* by Richard Kennedy, a sad tale of a rural eccentric fiddler, who covers his face with a cloth when appearing in public, as a symbol of grief after the death of his wife. He finally removes the veil when asked to play at the wedding of a friend's daughter.

A teacher one year from retirement had remained almost invisible during the two weeks, participating in the least obvious of ways. But she had been watching me carefully, and the techniques I was employing, as I was to discover.

In groups of threes, the teachers were to conduct an interview in role with Oliver Hyde and two councilors from town who were going to expropriate his small farm for a highway. The goal of the two players who were in role as the councilors was to persuade the player who was Oliver Hyde to remove a paper bag covering his/her head. One by one, the paper bags were removed, and the players then congregated by the teachers still in the midst of the drama. Eventually, there was one Oliver Hyde remaining, and the group of teachers stood around quietly as the last pair attempted to persuade her to remove the mask. She said nothing, simply sitting there silently while the interviewers struggled to see the hidden face. Soon, those who had been observing began questioning Oliver Hyde, with no result. In role, I joined in:

"We have no business being here, do we, Oliver? You have every right to determine the way in which you will live your life. If I had any choice, I would not be here. The highway is going through, no matter what we do here today. What can I do to make it easier for you? Can you help me to help you?"

She slowly lifted off the paper bag and she was weeping softly. Nobody talked for a moment, and then she laughed quietly and said that she was fine, and we all relaxed and sat together in a circle. She wrote me for several years after this experience, and each letter was more open than the last. In print, we dialogued over time and space, and she gave me strength to both wear the paper bag and take it off. She was one year from retirement when I met her. Just beginning another life. It is never too late. I hadn't planned on this particular drama, but the work allowed it to happen.


PAPER BAG MEMORIES

This lesson required some preplanning with a group of thirty teachers in Chicago. Because of the background of the children, who were seventh and eighth grade students studying musical theatre at a summer school, I felt the teachers should begin by sharing a story, and so groups of teachers practised retelling a tall tale, *The Snake-Bit Hoe Handle* by Doc McConnell. I had asked them to establish a context for a retelling to the children that would somehow involve them — a quilting bee, corn shucking, washing and so on. Then, the next morning, I taught them the words to a song from *Oliver Hyde's Dishcloth Concert* we would attempt to build upon:

> Oliver Hyde is a strange old man,
> He sticks his head in a coffee can,
> And hides his face when there's folks about,
> He's outside in, and he's inside out.

We were accompanied by a teacher on course, a gifted musician playing several instruments throughout the day, including the kinnor, which King David supposedly played.

We began by listening to the musician's songs and relating the images created in our minds by the sounds of the kinnor. Interestingly, the children conjured up ideas from King Arthur, the Bible and what they called "songs from the farms and hills." It was a quick step to the next phase of the work, with groups of four or five children listening to teachers retelling the tall tale from the day before, only this time the teachers were asked to dramatize the story in role, painting a picture of the Ozark community that would eventually contain the drama. As well, the teachers in role invited the youngsters to become members of mountain families, using mimed tasks to involve them.

We all joined a large circle and sang the "Oliver Hyde chant" that had been rehearsed earlier, accompanied by the musician, another teacher playing washboard, and free-form folk dancing. Teachers and children were all involved. Next, in groups of five, the teachers and the children created small tableaux, each group making two photographs for a community scrapbook that included Oliver Hyde — one serious picture and one "out-take" from the back of the album. One group at a time viewed the other frozen pictures and discussed their ideas and opinions about the context of each tableau they had seen. When we had all shared our tableaux, "Oliver Hyde" was removed from each of the photographs (one child per tableau). As narrator, I informed the class that this person, Oliver Hyde, had not been a part of this town for years. He now sat at home with a paper bag over his head, and we didn't know why. Each student playing Oliver Hyde was given a paper bag and sat apart from the class, trying on their masks.

The small groups had to decide why Oliver had been in hiding, and then share with the large group the rumors or stories they had created about him. To strengthen their work, as teacher in role, I said to all: "I want Oliver at my wedding. He once saved my life. He will come out tonight for one hour to your homes to speak with you. You must help me convince him to come to the wedding, take the bag off his head and play his fiddle." The small groups had to decide on a strategy that would convince each child in role as Oliver. This took almost thirty minutes.

Each Oliver met with his small group twice, and could only respond to their persuasions by nodding or shaking his head, as each child in role as Oliver wore a paper bag over his or her head. After half an hour of intensive questioning, none of the children had yet removed their masks. In role as the bridegroom, I asked each Oliver in turn to come to the wedding. I offered that the bride and I would wear paper bags to match his. I then said to all the children in role as Oliver: "Will you take your mask off, Oliver?" The tension was high as we waited for each child to respond. One by one, each Oliver Hyde made a personal decision, and in this case, all the students took off their bags. In celebration, the whole group danced to live music at the wedding, incorporating the song we had sung at the beginning of the drama. A teacher even performed a clog dance for us, as we clapped along with the music. A child and I, as bride and groom, danced in the circle as the drama closed.

I knew the day before that the drama lesson had to follow the genre of musical theatre, as the students felt that to be their mandate for the summer. As teacher, I wanted them to centre their work on the story they were creating, and to use the other arts to strengthen their drama. I remember vividly the storytelling session of *The Snake-bit Hoe Handle* by the teachers in groups to begin the lesson, and I still wonder at the freshness and energy they added to their retellings. Every group created a different setting for the tale, and every setting painted the stage for our drama. The musician was a wonder, improvising his tunes to our needs at the moment, underscoring our work, and counterpointing our rhythms. The paper bags used as masks were a powerful symbol for our work. Moments like this are few and far between. One teacher commented on the advantages of our exercises:

David needed time to choose students to pull out of groups to become Oliver. Tableaux gave this time to him to observe the children.

I suddenly had the realization that the student removed was Oliver, and that he was such an outsider — but he left a hole in the picture — almost like someone had cut him out.

I must say this was my favorite lesson. I felt the final moment of everyone dancing around on the floor to the glorious music was a wonderful celebration for the ending of the story but also of the whole creation process. The two young people I had the honor of working with were very involved, committed, and felt empathy for the story. They understood the soul of the drama. The young girl Lucia came up with the idea that Oliver Hyde's wife had died, and that Oliver was "ashamed." She thought of this idea, and expressed it, even though the teachers in the group were very overpowering. She was the one that would bring us back to the soul of the story, she found the emotion, she empathized with Oliver.

I finally understood that I should let the work be my focus, not my fear that the child may not be involved or that my deepening ability could harm the drama. Trust the work, and the children will give what they can give, and the teacher will give what she can give. The outcome can be very exciting...

## PLANNING DRAMA ACTIVITIES

Story drama work may last as little as five minutes, or as long as a month. The time will depend on the teacher's understanding of drama, the relationships the teacher can see between drama and other curriculum goals, and the teacher's readiness to take risks.

Drama can be either taught as a subject on the timetable or used as a learning medium in various areas of the curriculum — language arts, social sciences, physical education, music or art. Roleplaying allows children to experience some of the physical and emotional aspects of any topic, and deepens their understanding of course content. Understanding of group organization and dynamics, and skill in interpersonal relationships, can be reinforced through drama. Art, music and drama together form a powerful combination that can ignite perception and thought. Many aspects of a physical education program can reinforce, and are reinforced by, drama.

The right choice and management of situations, contexts and

stories relating to the environment, for instance, can provide young people with very authentic experiences of what it would be like to be in surroundings which might be far removed in time and place from their own. Drama deals with concrete and specific contexts — particular people in a particular relationship in a particular place at a particular time. Teachers need to take into account the nature of the children, their experience, their needs, their abilities and their interests. The teachers must choose from a repertoire of drama techniques and strategies, employing each convention toward the building of the collaborative drama activity.

The primary aim of drama should be to help children extract new meanings from their experiences and to communicate those meanings in the form of efficient, coherent responses. In this sense drama is both a subject matter and an approach to teaching of inherent value, particularly to the school curriculum.

# 4

## *The King and I*
### (A Model for Story Drama)

A librarian friend first gave me the book *The King's Fountain* twenty-five years ago, and I have been happily trapped in it ever since. Surely it is the vast possibilities that constantly draw me to it as a source for drama, a story so bare yet so intense that it seems totally unexplored every time I consider it as a beginning point for learning in role. A simple tale by Lloyd Alexander, illustrated by Ezra Jack Keats, echoing stories of desert tribes and powerful kings, it leaves magical spaces for children to fill in, like a tapestry worn in parts by time; our eyes struggle to find completeness, to grasp the whole picture.

A king wishes to build a fountain "for the splendor of his kingdom and the glory of his name." However, this would take all of the water from the village at the foot of the palace hill, causing suffering and despair to the people. An old man attempts to persuade others to speak to the king, but they all offer excuses, and his daughter suggests that he himself must make the journey up to the palace. Keats paints a rugged terrain, with a great chasm between the man and the king, and the subsequent meeting of the two results in the king's not building the fountain. That is the story, but as in all folktales, including this contemporary renewal of the form, the reader must bring to the text a world of context and understanding, and drama allows us to create a collaborative experiencing of story, creating a single tapestry of our group responses to the tale. No two creations will be alike; every group's efforts seem connected but separate, and yet each begins with the same narrative. After all these years, I have never lost interest in this story, for the very nature of improvised drama means that every experience will follow a different path, dependent upon the context of the group at that time. I am the storyteller, but in time, in role, they will tell me their story. All of us in the class are necessary to the storymaking, as we engage in filling in between the lines, digging within the words, arguing about such textual intent. We build our own story, and in the end it may not resemble *The King's Fountain* in structure, but all the accrued understandings of the tale will be woven into our creation.

This book is one of my most important sources for drama teaching, with dozens of lessons for children of all ages, about the feelings engendered in us by the author and the illustrator, and our attempts to give form and voice to those feelings. How will I know which road to follow with each group? This is the drama teacher's struggle — listening, watching, setting up situations that will foreshadow the direction of the journey, knowing when to intervene, when to use a particular strategy to open up discussion, to move the children into action, to cause them to pause, to reflect, to rethink, and all this without predetermining the learning, the content, the meat of the lesson. We provide the plasticene for them to model, and in drama, we will sculpt together, each move affecting all others, the individual finding strength from the group, and the group enriching and extending each individual. I'm afraid I spend little time in "one-on-one" in drama teaching, for having sensed the power of the group, I want to unleash it so that children can together create a play that, perhaps without audience, will reveal the thrill of theatre, of using improvised dialogue to build our sense of story. They will know when we have completed our work, and they will recognize the aesthetic power of theatrical collaboration.

When they have heard the tale, what will the children say? What will they take as their beginning points? What will they reveal about their lives and attitudes? Who will lead and who will support those leaders? What will I as teacher do throughout the lesson to deepen their sensibilities, clarify their inconsistencies, alter their conceptions, frame their learning? So many questions arise from such a brief book: this simple legend compresses many concepts into a brief narrative, and the following questions have been generated by dozens of classes in their attempts to understand the complexities of this archetypal situation. Each question the children ask, every comment they make, all the concerns I raise, give me insight into how I may want to construct the lesson: perhaps a game to open up energy, to initiate ideas, a technique such as creating a tableau to highlight a significant moment. As in all teaching, we watch, wait and suggest, letting the connections emerge, the learning develop. No twenty-minute lesson for drama — we need the hour, the day, the year. Our content will be the beginning, but the lessons will grow on their own, in their own shape and time. The following represent just a fraction of the questions discussion led to after I had read the story to classes of teachers and children. Your students will come up with questions of their own. The list is potentially endless.

Where did the story take place?
Did the king have a wife, a queen?
Why were there no female adults portrayed in the story?
What was the king's name? The old man's? The girl's?
Why did the king want to build the fountain?
Why had the village relied upon a single source of water for its very life?
What were the king's true motives in building this fountain?
Is there another way the king could show his glory to the people?
What kind of king was he? Benevolent? Autocratic? Wealthy?
How did the people feel about the king?
Where were the king's advisors in all of this?
What was the population of the village?
How many soldiers did the king have?
How do you represent visually the trappings of power?
Why were the wise people afraid to go to the king?
What was so intimidating about the king that no one would approach him?
Had an event like the building of the fountain happened in the past?
Was the king selfish, or just ignorant?
What happened in the king's past that made him think that it was appropriate to take away the village's water?

How did the villagers earn their livelihoods?
Why was the old man chosen to go to the king? (Were there no village advisors? No council?)
Why was there no water?
Why was the old man allowed to stand before the king when he was captured?
What did the old man say to the king? What tactics did the old man use to convince the king?
What did the little girl say/do? What was her role in the story? Was it the child's words that changed the king's mind?
What did the girl say to inspire her father to speak with the king?

## PROBLEM-SOLVING THROUGH DRAMA

Problem-solving is the basis of my improvisational drama work. The children are asked to express their response to a conflict through movement and talk. They are challenged to look at what is taking place for clues to the resolution of the conflict. Decisions about how a problem could be resolved are best reached during the drama, when the children in role are most intensely involved in the fictional situation. The most meaningful solutions will emerge while the children are immersed in their roles as co-operators, planners, decision-makers and, ultimately, problem-solvers.

One energetic first-grade group explored the need for water in our world. Extrapolating from their real-life roles as powerless children to the villagers in the drama, they opted to take gifts to the king, in an attempt to dissuade him from building the fountain. In small groups with student teacher scribes, they brainstormed suggestions for offerings for the ruler, and then, moving into action drama, they rehearsed how each family would present its tributes, as I offered some prompts as tension to help them build their scenes:

Will everyone go forward to meet the king or will an emissary be chosen?
Will they show defiance or respect?
How will they approach the throne?
What if each family unit gives a similar gift?
Shall we watch each other's groups to clarify our own strategy?

How will we support each other in the presence of this despot? Do we need any special costumes or objects?

After the general hubbub of practice, we were ready to meet the king. Fortunately, I could work inside the learning as teacher in role, focusing the drama, elevating the language, adding tension clarifying actions — but not predetermining outcomes. I selected to roleplay the king, since as a visitor to the classroom, I could play upon my lack of identity, and the students could use their social group as a safety network. How would I use surprise and tension to provoke thoughtful response — my constant quest.

By sitting on a chair on top of the teacher's desk, I literally elevated the power of the king, and changed the spatial arrangement of the class into a physical relationship between subjects and ruler. I needed to say very little, as my position directed the flow of dialogue. The groups, in turn, made their way up an aisle created by the children and the teachers, a theatrical form to heighten their sense of presentation. Such tributes were mimed — a cloak lined with rubies and diamonds, a throne of gold and silver, a crown of emeralds, a bag of coins — and each one turned down by the king: "I have all of that now. What I want is a fountain."

More small group work, the struggle for gifts with more substance, the beginnings of the power of symbols in changing attitudes. Once more, the presentations to the king, but this time, a villager cradling a baby in her arms.

"What are you offering me?"
"My child, your highness."
"I have children of my own."
"This baby has a star on her forehead, and can predict the future."
"Stand over here, then, beside me."

What deepened their work now was the opportunity to rework or relive the experience, the realization that the king had everything already, the time that allowed for gestation of ideas. In the final group presentation, a strong young girl marched boldly up the aisle, and shouted:

CHILD: O King, do not build the fountain.
DB: And why not?

CHILD: Because *he* says not to!

And from the back of the room came a boy with his eyes closed as if he were blind, his arms outstretched.

DB: What do you want, Blind Man?
CHILD: I have a message for the king.

*(He presented me with a small scroll, held by a hairband.)*

DB: You can neither read nor write.
CHILD: It came to me in a dream.

*(I opened the paper and read:)*

O King, be a good king.

Of course, the fountain would not be built, and the cheers of the children evidenced the duality of role — pride in working as a grade one class in conquering a complex problem, and the success of a village in thwarting the insensitive dictates of an unfair ruler. Drama lives in that dichotomy of role — the self and the other as they blend. That class cheered for childhood's future victory and drama's power, and *The King's Fountain* was rewritten, retold, relived, remembered.


LETTERS TO THE KING

One teacher's specialty was visual arts, but she came to my drama class with an open mind and a desire to integrate the two modes of artistic expression. And yet, the results were written composition. When teachers work in role for the first time, it is often a shocking experience. Many trivialize the work, protecting their images, thinking that drama needs to be funny. This group of teachers in Detroit was no exception, and I, as group leader, needed to let the energy begin to coalesce, building each experience into a stronger whole. It amazes me to watch experienced, mature teachers working in role, their insecurities with this artform, the volume of their voices, the need they seem to have for violent confrontations, punctuated by outbursts of hysterical laughter. This is always true to form, depending upon the experience level of the participants. I have been knocked to the ground by a teacher roleplaying with what he felt was "real violence," and mocked as a "short four-eyes" by a teacher who had no conception of a person in role. And yet when they grasp hold of the medium, they do possess great talent and power. I have collected all sorts of role games that require listening to a partner or to a small group, and reacting as opposed to acting, until the members feel safe enough to let the self mesh with the other to create role. As one particular teacher began to improvise, to roleplay, to sense the strength in working within the structure, her work grew in only one week to where I knew she was a drama teacher.

Having explored *The King's Fountain* with this group of teachers, I was not surprised to find her choosing that text as her unit for the required project in her own school. But I cannot forget the results of her own classroom work, when she brought in the findings of her exploration to share with her colleagues. Her grade four class had chosen to write to the king as village tribal elders, and she assisted them as the one who supplied the materials. And what letters! She told us that the point of departure in the story for her children was the old man's fear that his language was not equal to the king's, and their subsequent work was based on the attempts of the villagers to use elevated, formal language structures. The letters that follow demonstrate her strengths as an art teacher as well, as the children used calligraphy on parchment, illuminating their initial letters, and struggling to find the words and the syntax appropriate for addressing a king.

Dear King,

Your town, which soon faces destruction, is asking you if you would stop the building of the fountain. If you won't stop, we have some reasons why you should. Most of the people are too old to walk twenty miles to get water that their families need. The children are too young to get the water because they don't know their way to the east and the wild animals might kill them. The merchants want more for getting the water and want the poor to pay for that water.

Dear King,

My people in the village below you, hear you are making a fountain in front of your castle and we also hear it will take up all of our water for our pets, produce, and us. So, if you make a fountain in front of your castle, we won't be able to come every day because it is so far and we will die. So, if we die, you will have no one to rule or be kind to. So, please don't make your fountain. You won't regret it.

Sincerely,
Villagers

Dear King,

I write to complain about the water. I think it is nice that you want to make a fountain. But we do get water now. What about later if all the young members of the town go to work? Then we can't get it and it's always late at night. And they won't get it, they are tired. They will just get enough for themselves. I think you should make a stream going through the town.

Tim

I am amazed at these letters and aware of this teacher's great strengths in the classroom. She began with a story she had heard, helped the children develop a form of expression, and supported their attempts to find aesthetic and linguistic means to influence those in power. This last letter, however, remains my favorite — poorly written, but with brutal, honest strength.

Dear King,

Your fountain is dum. It does nothing but kill people and when you go get the water our village will die.

P.S. Knock it down.

That's all king.

David

I asked the teacher about this child, and she replied that his comprehension of the activity was high, but that he did not hear the music of the words. She felt he needed many more stories, and many more opportunities to represent and communicate his ideas. (And I had been afraid she might be concerned with his handwriting.) Good teachers new to drama quickly understand this way of teaching and learning, and seem to have little trouble in adapting its strengths for their own classrooms.

I want drama to deepen the children's understanding of themselves, others and where they live, as they build an improvised world through a process of group interaction. Although I encourage them to create imaginary gardens, their response to the problems, conflicts and characters must be real. How the teacher elicits both commitment and authenticity is what is important to true learning.

### THE POWER OF CHILDREN IN ROLE

STUDENT ONE: Listen here! Now there are two kings!

TEACHER IN ROLE: (*To new king*) What are you going to do?

STUDENT TWO: Get our water back!

STUDENT ONE: We heard that!

TEACHER IN ROLE: This imposter has come forward. Why have you come all this way?

STUDENT TWO: To get the water for our village and the animals.

STUDENT THREE: He is the true king! He has come to get the water back for our village!

STUDENT ONE: Should we make *him* a king or *him* a king?

STUDENT TWO: (*To Teacher in role*) You! Go find your own water and build your own fountain. Leave the village!

TEACHER IN ROLE: He has said I should leave and I shall. Stand and bow to the new king! And will you be a good king? What will you do for the people?

STUDENT TWO: Let them have the water back.

TEACHER IN ROLE: (*To guard*) Will you come with me or will you stay in the village?

STUDENT ONE: I will stay with you because you are the best king!

TEACHER IN ROLE: What will we do in the new land?

STUDENT ONE: Build a new fountain and a new castle. I will guard the new fountain. I'll sleep out there to guard it. And we will build two fountains so they will check the wrong one!

These were spontaneous drama words of a group of grade one children who were being filmed while taking part in a drama lesson. In role as king, I had attempted to develop in the class a sense of responsibility for determining their own fate as a nation. I had for this part of the film chosen my role to encourage an immediate talk-filled situation, and the students had gradually decided that they no longer wished to be ruled by such a leader. One boy, Student Two, assumed the role of a new king who deposed me with the support of the people and ordered me from the kingdom. His language, in every respect, was that of the one in charge: there was no mere pretending to be a ruler. The dynamic of the classroom had altered. As a result, Student Two was able to speak as king. His language demonstrates the freedom and strength that can emerge in this type of learning, when drama words happen in a classroom.

## WORKING WITHOUT A NET

In a large school auditorium in Chicago, a group of third and fourth grade boys and girls sat with me as we discussed the rain outside, and the need for moisture for the land if drought was to be avoided. The children offered comments about the ecological balance that had to be maintained for a necessary food supply in a country where water was scarce. Taking my idea from the book we had not yet shared, *The King's Fountain*, I asked them why a leader might want to encourage a drought. The children became American reporters in a country in the Middle East, attempting to search for the reasons behind the leader's actions. Here is what one teacher wrote of the demonstration session:

> Our discussion on the beginnings of lessons interested me. I am concerned about having everyone's attention, and I do not always trust the work to give it to me. I will try to monitor my feelings about this point next year.
>
> It was great being in role with another teacher because we could play off each other without giving the children direct information...
>
> This was a group ready to explode! They were truly thinkers. The close, quiet discussion of rain, water and drought was intense and varied. The strongly worded question of "Why would a man or woman want to make a drought?" plunged them to the heart of the drama and resulted in a wide range of responses from accidental pollution, to something having to do with "40 days and 40 nights." They were not afraid to challenge David, as when he came up with a reason and they all shouted, "Ahh, that's not true!"
>
> I liked the fact that we (the adults) were told the day prior to meeting these students that we were not to give them any direct information, that we were supposed to speak in riddles... This lesson was a perfect example of doing story drama without ever

reading or telling the story to the children. After a discussion which started with the fact that it was raining outside and how some people pray for rain because of drought, the children were told that, "Today in our drama there's going to be a very bad drought." They were also assigned their roles by David: "You are from another country..." ("American!" was called out by a patriotic young boy.)

"... and you are reporters who have been chosen by the UN to find out what is happening in the east and why there is a terrible drought."

In pairs, the children interviewed small groups of teachers in role as villagers, who had been asked to appear reluctant to reveal any information to outsiders. The children then reported back to me any knowledge about the situation they had discovered. To deepen their roles, I had requested that the reporters offer the villagers a drink from their canteens, and try to win their confidence. For my part in the drama, I chose to remain as side-coach, out of role but inside the drama.

This group was interesting to me because of the use of language to get information. The role of the children as investigators deepened the drama quickly and the quality of belief was high. My partner and I had the good fortune of having a boy who had been described as developmentally delayed. He was so into the drama, so sincere, so concerned about helping the villagers that the depth of the work we could do was incredible. Questioning and asking for information were important uses of language in this lesson and effective for building belief. In the children's work with David, they had to give lots of explanations of how and why things were happening, of projecting and comparing possible alternatives and or reflecting on feelings, especially of the village people they had interviewed.

After the subsequent interviews, I removed the children from the auditorium while the teachers created a living fountain as a group theatre exercise. The child reporters then returned to view the mysterious factor causing the drought.

On this day my insecurities really came out. I found I was constantly judging my deepening choices. The young person I was with was also having difficulty staying in role as the reporter. Or, perhaps, I was asking all the questions, to try to get her to stay in role. I understand the concept of tensions and deepening. However, I need to trust myself more and to trust the children. I kept asking myself, "Will what I just did hinder the drama?" I have to remember the only thing that will hinder the drama is my insecurity. Trust the work.

In the next scene in our drama work, the villagers shared with the reporters a prepared riddle concerning an eagle, which, through discussion, the children interpreted as a helicopter that the leader used to survey and control his people. After the children and I left the room once more, the teachers built, through collaborative movement, a helicopter with rotating blades and sound effects, and when the reporters witnessed its landing in the desert, they confirmed their suspicions of a military leader who was telling untruths to his people.

The two machines we created were fun for me. I was able to release some of my energy. So often I am out of the play. This was my time to play. I did not realize how menacing our giant human helicopter was until the children came in and screamed.

As the bell rang, the drama drew to a close, with the children as reporters choosing to leave their fictional country because of imminent war.

This lesson was free-form in design, and troublesome by its nature for many teacher-participants. Never as teacher have I been more secure with a lesson, knowing that I could call upon my hundreds of experiences with *The King's Fountain* over two decades. I must remember with teachers new to drama that they don't have my classroom experiences as a template for forming new lesson directions. I was able to share with these teachers the strength of having fairly developed lesson ideas with which to begin the drama, but I had no definite route mapped out. However, I have been on a thousand journeys reminiscent of this one, and I have relished the twists and turns on the way.

## A Model for Story Drama

| | | | |
|---|---|---|---|
| The Story | Personal Anecdote<br>Folktale<br>Novel<br>Picture Book | Report<br>Poem/Song<br>Film | Short Story<br>Excerpt |
| Experiencing the Story | Read to the children.<br>Read by the children.<br>Created by the children. | Seen on film/video by the children.<br>Told by a guest teacher.<br>Read from the children's experiences. | |
| Creating Drama from the Story | Explore the issues within the story before meeting the text.<br>Create the drama from the implications of the story in the lives of the children.<br>Develop parallel or analogous situations that draw from the energy of the story.<br>During the story experience, stop at a problem to be solved or a decision to be taken.<br>Extend the story back in time or forward into an imagined future.<br>Elaborate upon the subtext of the story.<br>Invent unwritten scenes referred to in the story.<br>Build the drama from the children's responses to the story.<br>Explore the characters, their motivations and relationships.<br>Add or expand minor characters, altering the direction of the story drama.<br>Examine story incidents from a new perspective.<br>Present additional problems or alter events.<br>Use the story's emotional qualities to create a new environment.<br>Enact the story to depict or demonstrate a significant issue.<br>Have the children read the story aloud as participants to restore voice to the text. | | |

# A Model for Story Drama (cont'd)

| | |
|---|---|
| The Teacher's Role | Structure the drama for maximum learning. Narrate moments within the drama, summarize or reflect on what happened. Side-coach the children individually or in groups as the drama is occurring. Work in role to direct the drama from within the action. Assess the work in progress and redirect the learning. Work as a teacher/artist, shaping and guiding the feelings and ideas of the children. Select from a variety of techniques strategies to co-construct the drama. |
| The Children's Role | Explore ideas and feelings co-operatively and collaboratively. Live through the drama moments. Depict and demonstrate significant issues. Reveal and share insights. Work alone, in groups and as an ensemble. Connect the fiction to personal experiences. Make private and public meanings by committing to the work. Respond to and communicate with others. Roleplay and storytell within the frame of drama. Read aloud their own words and the words of others within the drama. Represent ideas and feelings in various media. Understand and employ the sense of theatre power. Reflect on both self and art. |
| Techniques and Strategies | Games and activities · Visual arts<br>Parallel story sets · Mask-making<br>Supportive research · Problem-solving<br>Choral reading · Decision-making<br>Movement · Rituals and ceremonies<br>Dance drama · Flashbacks and<br>Storytelling · flashforwards<br>Writing in role · Foreshadowing<br>Teacher in role · Frozen pictures |

## A Model for Story Drama (cont'd)

| Techniques and Strategies (cont'd) | A guest in role<br>Working with another class<br>Thought-tracking<br>Narrative by the teacher<br>Pair work<br>Small group work<br>Ensemble work | Use of video, photographs<br>Finding a specific site<br>Interviews<br>Hot-seating in role<br>Children as experts |
|---|---|---|

# 5

## *Becoming a Tribe*
### (Building a Classroom Community)

Willi Baum, the author/illustrator of the picture book *The Expedition*, has used a series of pictures in a cartoon fashion to tell his story about a tribe on an island, and the events that occur when another people arrive. The reader enters a new world and constructs a society that is only hinted at, never seen in actuality. The story drama lies in developing these unknown people — their life, their work, their tribal celebrations, their lives and the conflict that results when strangers representing another culture arrive in their land. Because the people on the island are not pictured, we can develop their lives and their civilization as the basis for roles in story drama. "How will their lives be different from our own?" "What will their beliefs be?" "What will they believe about the seasons, the sun or the new visitors?"

Many teachers are unsure they will be able to draw their students into drama, but taking time to speculate, to work on ideas, to imagine together, can bring spectacular results.

In order to develop the role of the tribe, we can decide on some of the important rituals in their lives. One picture shows a temple that has been dismantled. "What could it have been used for?" "Would it have to do with sickness or the seasons, celebrating war or honoring family ceremonies such as birth or death?"

Working in groups of five and six, the children in a grade six class created one of the rituals that would have gone on in the temple long ago. I played a recording of Paul Horne to create a suitable atmosphere. The groups worked simultaneously, and I assisted when necessary. The rituals were all religious in nature, based on archetypes from the children's own experiences.

I led the groups into a circle to represent the temple, and narrated the children through their demonstrations of the rituals, questioning them about their ceremonies. For example, one group had raised someone from death by plague: "Would a plague victim have been alive if the new world had brought medicine to the island?"

Next, the children sat in a circle and one by one volunteers narrated the story of the islanders' first encounter with visitors, as it was told yearly by the tribe in order to represent the dangers of outsiders finding their island.

In role as a tourist leader, I addressed the class as the tribe, whose temple had been desecrated. I promised to bring them the inventions of civilization if they agreed to my plans to develop the island as a tourist centre. In groups, the children discussed the reasons they would give a visitor for refusing or accepting my offer. Next, in whole-class discussions in role, and in spite of my attempts to persuade the children to accept the conveniences of the contemporary world, the children struggled with the dilemma, the girls wanting the new technology, and the boys refusing to be subjugated by an outside force.

The class was extremely agitated about having to make a decision, and left the room debating the problem: "Will he ruin the bird sanctuary?" "Will the beaches be destroyed with oil spills?"

I returned the following week and the children's energy was still focused. They had to vote on accepting or rejecting the tourism proposal; I gave each member two marbles — a white one for yes, a red for no — and each child went to the centre of the circle and placed the marble of choice in a dish. The tribe rejected the modern world.

I received this letter two weeks later from the student who had acted as spokesperson.

Dear Mr. Booth,

When we were talking about The Expedition, you asked us if we would let you come to our island, and bring civilization. You explained that meant building us hospitals, giving us technology, but in the same time you will have to cut down some of our trees, build casinos and bring in unknown diseases.

I had no objection to this proposition, but I did not like the idea of you destroying the environment on our island.

At the very end of our discussion you said, "Fine, I will leave you alone, but sooner or later other nations will find out about your island and come to you with war instead of peace." This started me thinking.

In conclusion to the discussion, there is only one result: we will give you our knowledge, some of our gold and natural resources. In return you will give us your knowledge, electricity and protection from other countries that want to wage war on us.

Yours truly,
Andrei

He had changed his mind. Why? What had happened when I left? Did the drama continue? What pressures were brought to bear? Did Andrei actually reflect by himself on what had happened and rethink his own view of the problem?

Slowing down the work enables the children to consider its implications thus far. Through a rehearsal, such as the building of the temple histories, or through foreshadowing future events, we can allow a class to channel its energy without damaging the potential for genuine drama to take place.

### "PEOPLE-MAKERS"

The following information may help you draw up the first plans for developing two tribes — the indigenous and the newly arrived — but bear in mind that it can be adapted for almost any introductory session about story drama. By asking questions and drawing the children into discussion, problem-solving and other group activities, you are also inevitably involving them in the coming drama.

The class is going to create two separate groups of people — two tribes. Each tribe will be developed by one-half of the class, who will make all decisions concerning the people they are creating. Once each tribe has been developed and the drama has grown through improvisation, you can share your creation with the other half of the class.

In the course of discussion each group can revise the roles, and the other group can depict its tribe for an audience in role.

As one group watches the other, you must help the children as an involved audience with their own roles by asking questions such as:

Will they be anthropologists studying the tribe?
Will they be scientists attempting to cure deadly diseases?
Will they be a futuristic tribe?
Will they come from the past?
Will they be hidden from the passage of time?

For the sake of the drama you will have to all speak English, but each time the tribe is being depicted, you can use a distinctive style of speaking or incorporate mime into your work.

The audience will have to observe the actors closely to attempt to learn as much as possible about the tribe, so that in their report at the conclusion of the drama experience, they can reveal, in role, what they have found. This means that the actors will have to be aware of the audience and take into account what they are seeing and making sense of. In this way, you will be working within the artform of drama to communicate with an audience.

In building a people in drama, you can explore many aspects of life using these sources of information: work, worship, business, communication, clothing, education, family, food, health, law, leisure, shelter, travel, war.

However, drama is more than simply portraying any one aspect of life; it is working your way through the many problems and situations that arise when you are living in the real world, no matter where or when. Each aspect of life can be broadened or made specific through drama.

If "food," for instance, is the focus of the tribe, you can demonstrate:

a) how food is found (it is through fishing, trapping, hunting or the gathering of plants and berries?);
b) who does the locating of food;
c) who prepares the food;
d) who distributes the food;
e) what happens in a famine.

Similarly, each aspect of life can be depicted and used as the basis for the drama to come. In order to give focus to the drama, the teacher may choose one aspect at a time to explore. For example, the tribe may create a ritual to celebrate spring. In this way, you and your group members will be building up a picture of a whole people — their behavior, values, relationships and rituals — so that this information can be shared with another group who are meeting this tribe for the first time.

## WORKING ALONE AND WITH OTHERS

Drama should involve as many children as possible. Generally, it is best if all the children are involved at the same time in experimenting with the flow of thinking, the flow of language and the flow of movement.

Sometimes the children will work separately without interacting with others. This provides an opportunity for deepening concentration, allows privacy for individual exploration and minimizes distractions. The class can work as a single unit, with each individual functioning as a part of the whole.

Sometimes the children will work in pairs or in small groups, stimulating each other's thinking and lending support to other members of the group. Each child needs to work with a variety of partners, and the tasks can be carefully designed. There need be little sharing, but groups can demonstrate or depict some of their findings, so that there is a sense of community rather than competition.

Sometimes the children work as a whole class, at a public forum — a meeting, a council, a seminar — everyone in role and everyone a part of the whole.

Some children seem to demand immediate and continuous involvement and need to be pressed into deeper achievement; others must be persuaded (not forced) to participate. We must continually accept their efforts and encourage them to extend their involvement. The meanings that will accrue in a child's life grow from personal involvement and experience.

While working with the children in various groups, I can play a different role with each group. As well, I can move about the room, questioning groups, challenging ideas, promoting deeper thought, communicating ideas between groups, resetting a problem, defining a focus.

I may structure the task-centred problem-solving in pairs or in small groups, encouraging child-to-child interaction, but I have learned that it is important to call the group back together to check on what has been happening. "What discussion has your group had?" "Did everyone agree?" "What caused your group to think this way?" "Do you agree with what the other groups have said?" The children must feel that what occurred during the group time was important to themselves and to the drama activity as a whole.

Drama is a corporate act; it involves the negotiation of meaning between individuals with different views of what is being worked on in the drama. The teacher assists the class, building a contract where all the participants are making conscious and deliberate decisions in the safety of fictional role. The greatest growth in the children's understanding of thoughts and feelings of people in the drama situation occurs when the whole class is working together, and where the small group work helps deepen the drama for the whole class experience.

There are so many ways to let group work play a part in the growth of whole class drama:

- each group may report back to the whole class in role (or choose a spokesperson, such as an elder);
- each group may show a moment of learning they have arrived at, in tableau or in depicting a special incident; several groups may volunteer to demonstrate some aspect of their learning;
- the groups may recreate an incident which ocurred in the drama experience;
- the individuals, in a circle, may express in role their feelings about the group's activity;
- the teacher may freeze the starting point of the action of each group (it may not be beneficial to show all the work of each group to one another);
- the work that went on in groups can be the basis for the next part of the drama lesson as structured by the teacher; the group work may become a play within the larger context of the whole class drama experience, a play within a play.

Sometimes the children will simply observe and discuss. This does not mean they are a passive audience, but individuals who want to learn or glean information from the drama they are watching.

As the work progresses, and if the participants lack commitment or belief in the drama, the teacher can stop the action, question the children further and then begin the work again. At different points in the drama, the action can be stopped as groups report on what is happening, or the teacher can present alternative actions for exploration. The dynamic of the interaction structures the drama. I am always struggling to find the right technique for creating action, for building reflection or for demonstrating the collective power of the class. All variations in grouping are necessary — the child alone, the small group, the whole class. I need them all.

### REVISITING THE STORY

This year a fourth grade class in a tough urban setting created their own story drama with me from *The Expedition*. The young girl who roleplayed the tribe's leader demonstrated great solemnity and composure during our work. In these four letters, you will see the outgrowth of the class's reflections, helped by a fine teacher's writing program. Note the child as leader's two separate entries, the second one in response to her listening to the class debate in role the issue of whether to accept the restoration of the temple by foreigners. She has strengthened her belief in her own role and in the dramatic conflict, and her writing is powerful evidence of her learning.

Dear Captain,

It is me the leader of all my people. I have made my decision. It was very easy for me to make. My decision is going to be I will *not* take the temple from you because you seemed very strange and you were mean and why would you offer me my temple unless you are very sorry about what your grandfather did? I am *not* sorry about what I did to your grandfather. Thanks to your grandfather if he didn't take the temple I wouldn't take the top off your ship.

Your enemy,
The Leader

Dear Captain,

I agree with our leader not to take back our temple because I don't trust you and your king. Plus, what if it's a trap? We'll suffer even more. So don't bring back the temple.

(P.S. Throw that old looking temple into the deepest sea you can find.)

Your enemy,
The Cubby Man

Dear Captain,

I've made a decision. I disagree with the leader. I think that you should bring it back. The people are dying. There has been some mysterious drownings. People are catching the flu and diseases and we can't figure out why the babies are born so small. This is the reason why I want the temple back.

Yours truly,
Cinqaina

Dear Captain,

It is me again. As you can see, some people did not agree with me. One even wanted to overthrow me but the rest of my people didn't want the temple. So that means I am still the leader. Don't return to the island. My decision is made and my people agree with me and will stand by me. If you return, you will be hanged.

Still the Leader,
Power Woman

Would I had her strength and confidence in both her social position in the class and leadership inside the drama. When the children own the work, my role in the classroom becomes different. My energies can be devoted to strengthening those children on the edge, side-coaching them to enter the circle.

# 6

## Who's in Charge?
### (The Role of the Teacher)

### TEACHER ALONE

When something is always viewed from the same spot, it turns into boring old stuff ultimately ignored by the senses and not felt at all. Zooming in and out means changing your viewpoint. From the tree you can go on to experience either the leaf or the forest. From any substance you can go either in the direction of its atom or in the direction of its world, both having their corresponding orbits and consciousness.

*Zooming In*

I was in Hudson Bay several years ago, on an island called Sanikiluaq, working with teachers and Inuit children. I taught three groups, beginning with kindergarten and moving to grade eight. I had no idea I would find −40-degree weather on my arrival, and I was just wearing a trench coat. When I met the Inuit parents and children and leaders, they simply stared at me. The leader of the community rose and said, ''I wish to greet you but I haven't your skill in languages and I shall struggle to speak in English and do my best.'' And he was of course the most eloquent speaker I've ever heard. He then made the same speech in Inuit and I was embedded in the community for two weeks. I went seal hunting, ice fishing, skidooing, partying — and I taught drama. If you ever want to have yourself thrown into using only what you are, try working on Hudson Bay.

When I walked into the first class of children, they all began speaking in Inuit among themselves, and I knew I was a foreigner, an alien, a stranger, a distrusted one. And I had no idea how to begin or where to start. Everything, every warm-up I've ever thought of, died in that −40-degree weather. My glasses, by the way, in the four minutes it took to get to the school, would frost over so heavily I had to scrape them before I could see. I was trapped in this room. I decided I would move right into drama. I had brought my case of books, thinking I would begin with myths and legends, but none of them seemed to apply to where I was at the moment. "Tell me about your community," I said. And they all roared with laughter because it was only as big as this room, with 200 students and 300 adults. They had all known their community from the day they were born. And they had never left. "Why do we want to bother taking time to talk about our community?" "Because I'm a stranger and I want to know a little bit about it." And so they began. We listed on the blackboard all the important places — the Hudson's Bay store, the co-op, the recreation centre, the school, the Mountie station, the nurse's clinic and so on. Then I said, "If I were a government official sent to your community to eliminate one service building, which one would you choose?" They had a discussion for an hour and a half. I watched girls who could not speak to me begin whispering to each other across the room. We began erasing the buildings, one by one, when we had a consensus, until only the Hudson's Bay Store was left. I was in the middle of their drama, totally controlled by them, using all the strategies I'd learned in my world. From then on, I had no trouble.

After the final gathering at the teacher's house a group of Inuit built an icehouse for me, an igloo, built into the ground. They put a lamp in it, and I entered the house as it glowed from the inside. It was such a powerful place; you felt the North around you, inside you. Later, when I was walking home, there was no wind and the stars were out. It was breathtaking, free of all urban industrial grime. And at midnight, in the middle of this island, in the middle of Hudson Bay, on a snow-covered hill, I heard a fourteen-year-old adolescent Inuit boy, all by himself, singing Bruce Springsteen's "Born in the USA." I realized that I had been there, on their island, trying to learn about them, and for decades we had been flooding and filtering into their world. That boy wasn't singing to me, he was singing to him-

74

self and to the spirits of his island. He was in the middle of a theatre experience. He was full of drama, and I was moved.

When I was leaving for my airplane, a teenager handed me a poem, which he said was his only one, and he wanted me to have it.

Musk ox:
Hey Goose, can you find my wife for me?
I really need my wife. Do you know where my wife is? If
you tell me where my wife is, I will save you from the
hunter. I am suffering
for my wife.

Sea gull:
You'll never know where your wife is.
I married her yesterday.
She said she loved me.

Johnny

### THE TRICKS OF THE TRADE

How do we make drama happen? What are the techniques we can use to build its power, to increase its significance, so that the children recognize the value of their work? My colleague and friend Gano Haine and I were taking our graduate degrees with Gavin Bolton in England, and throughout the year's course we were required to work often in drama with children. I was struck by Gano's ability to use tension as a way of deepening, enriching and extending the drama. She has an amazing way of suddenly making us recognize the specifics of the drama. For example, in a medieval drama, children in grade five were trying to get their true king returned to them. They decided to be bird trainers, sending messages by carrier pigeon to the imprisoned king, and right away, through her questioning, her taking on role, her setting the specifics of the situation to be explored by partners, groups and the whole class, Gano made us see those pigeons in front of our eyes. We held them in our hands. Gano asked us about the preparations we must make before the pigeons were able to fly. She wanted to know who was in charge of tagging the pigeons, who would sweep the coop, who would feed the birds. She had us each hold an imaginary pigeon, to check its wings, to make sure that it would be able to fly with the message. As a village, we had to test the pigeons' abilities to see which one would be given the message, one and only one. We fed them and cared for them and made them real. Finally, Gano picked one imaginary pigeon feather from the floor, put it between the pages of her book and said, "In this feather is the freedom of our kingdom."

Tension is the secret, the mystery, the surprise, the dangling carrot, the time frame, the space limit. We need to apply pressures of some kind so that the children will know the urgency of solving the problem or of making the decision at hand. We can use a surprising or shocking experience. For example, we can foreshadow that one of the people in the great canoe will die. The shock may force the children into rethinking what they were going to do. We can pull the experience in the opposite direction to where it seems to be going. In a plan where the class in role were to take over a community by appearing in the early morning fog, we tell them the fog has disappeared, the sky is clear and we are in view of the enemy village. We can place special demands on the roleplayers: they will have to solve a riddle so they can gain the right to speak to the wise one; they will have to speak in a way that the king will accept, using carefully chosen language to influence him. As teachers, we can make things difficult for the children: only one person knows the combination for the safe, or the swans will return earlier than normal because of the eclipse of the sun. We can also ask children to become the experts in a field: those who have information on a particular animal that is almost extinct, or those who understand a people's culture on an island we are about to visit. One of the most significant tensions is to slow down the work deliberately by asking the children to reflect within the drama on what has happened. For example, we may see three plans enacted in order to choose only one of them; we can rehearse the battle with the monster so that we can check the state of our weapons; we can use a flashback or a flashforward to heighten the choices that we must make; we can require careful planning exercises using chart paper and markers.

What we want to do with these strategies is elevate the children's feelings and ideas, so that the ensuing drama will be stronger. We are creating an elaborate context for what has happened, not only responding in action but with reflection. Of course, by working in role as teachers we can offer many more tensions than we could if we were only at the front of the room. Just being able to say, "When I was a young child in this village, I remember something similar happening," adds other directions for the drama.

The learning in drama occurs with the experience of being involved directly; the children will have to think on their feet as participants. We must move them into areas of significance where they will meet learning challenges, yet not detract from their own part in shaping the drama. We must handle decisions concerning styles, strategies and activities, informed by the understandings of the children's needs at a particular time in a particular situation. They control the theme, either the choice or the direction, but we structure the content and decide the purpose for using and experiencing this theme. Their ideas are the important ones: my job is to organize, clarify and amplify these ideas. Although my chief goal is to give the children responsibility for their own learning, I retain responsibility for the structure and the organization of the lesson. By structuring the lesson, I can help the children see the implications behind their actions and an understanding of the "greater good" of the whole class. The drama rests upon the balance between what they want to do and my perceptions of the possibilities inherent in their drama. I see my job as helping the children find a focus for the drama that is acceptable to the majority of the class. However, I must not direct the drama or have the students follow orders. I try to control the situation without providing all the ideas, applying pressure and deepening the experience where necessary. It is a continual process of organization and reorganization, of focusing and refocusing. I must see the implications of every suggestion, then find an appropriate strategy for utilizing these ideas with the group.

I need to set up learning structures that allow for the spontaneity of the children, but engage them in a meaningful learning experience. I need to choose activities within the abilities of the group, yet stretch their developing capacities. Learning atmospheres need to be created where talk is healthy and normal, so that I can elicit constant response and support the contributions of each child. I want to challenge superficial responses, press for the elaboration and extension of inadequate contributions, but without rejecting the speakers themselves. I want to seek further information from the class without burdening them with my own knowledge. I must find structures to interest and motivate the group, encouraging them to explore rather than demonstrate what they already know. I need to use various modes of teaching to pace the work so that feelings and thoughts are encouraged to develop, carefully observing which attitudes and perceptions should be focused upon, and which are detrimental.

Jerome Bruner suggests that "the shrewd guess, the fertile hypothesis, the courageous leap to a tentative conclusion — these are the most valuable coin of the thinker at work, whatever his line of work." For this to happen, for thinking and feeling skills to be sharpened and used, a teacher's intervention is necessary, mandatory, a vital part of the teaching/learning process.

## THE CARETAKER IN ROLE

When I began teaching drama, my principal's advice included the adage, "Be good to the caretaker. He'll know all your secrets and control your future." Too true. I remembered my first drama lesson as a student in eighth grade, just after World War II. Emigrants from England were forced to take jobs that they had not been trained for. The principal/teacher knew our caretaker's background in theatre, and each Thursday afternoon, we were taught movement and drama by the man who cleaned the floors and scrubbed the toilets on Monday and Tuesday. His abilities caused us to respect him no less than our teacher, and the work progressed until parents' night when we demonstrated our "skeleton world," using "Danse Macabre" to help the adults see beyond our adolescent difficulties. I loved that evening; we touched on dance and drama, and it will be with me always. At the conclusion of the sharing, everyone drank Freshie and ate cookies and talked theatre, and at 10:00 p.m., we left, while the caretaker cleaned up after us, and was alone in his gymnasium with his broom and dustpan, alone in his theatre.

And what would our dragon play have been without another caretaker? We were conducting our drama program in a church hall, and the adults were having difficulty building belief in their own roles, which were inspired by tales of King Arthur's knights. It was hard for thirty adults on a hot July day in a church hall to make drama happen, and as I sweated and struggled, the caretaker came into the room to ask what time we would be

78

finished. Out of nothing but desperation, I asked him to find the truth within the dragon tapestries that had been discovered in a cave so that we could free a knight from the curse. And he stared, and walked around the tableau figures, and began to tell us what he saw. He had no teeth and no drama training, and he knew the secrets of that tapestry. When he left thirty minutes later, we gathered in our reflection circle and talked about status stereotypes and strangers entering our drama. We bought him a large bottle of scotch. (He didn't drink, of course. You need all your faculties to discover dragons.)

## THE TEACHER'S VOICE

And what of the teacher's own language arts? How important are our own skills in speaking and listening, reading and writing? What types of language behavior do we show our children during our time with them? Do they learn from us an unwritten curriculum in languaging by simply observing, interacting with and listening to us? Dorothy Heathcote feels that the language skills of teaching must be "honed in use and practice." She believes that teachers must be aware of the power that their language can bring to the drama and of the pleasure and inspiration this can be to children. The teacher must read aloud, if not with the skills of a trained voice, at least with an understanding of what is being read and with a determination to read it with integrity and commitment. We need to put words and spoken language to efficient use — selecting words carefully, powerfully, economically — to best fit the purpose of the experience.

Because story drama is a particular way of learning, the teacher requires a great sensitivity to language, so that the most possible can be revealed at any moment in the drama. As well, it is important to develop a good ear for language affect, a wide range of tone, effective volume and pitch and a well-controlled choice of vocabulary. This sounds challenging, but take heart! The children will lead us to the language source. By working inside the drama and alongside the children, by trying on different roles and voices in the safety of the drama experience, by actually caring about the content of the drama and by becoming passionately involved in the actions and reactions of the children — the teacher will learn with the children, take part in the journey and feel the rewards and satisfaction of education at its most significant.

If it is true that the most valuable language learning for participants happens when they are involved at a thinking/feeling level, then is it not true for the teacher/learner as well? While the play for the teacher and the play for the children may be different, the language needs remain constant: to communicate appropriately and effectively; to understand the needs of those listening and participating; and to be free enough to become involved in the making of meanings, both private and public. The teacher will be able to use different patterns of language as narrator and as roleplayer, freed from the traditional classroom patterns of interaction.

### LOOKING OUT FROM INSIDE

Working in role does not require much acting skill on the part of the teacher, but rather the adoption of a set of attitudes. As teacher, I work in the drama alongside the children, and they must know when I am in role. Perhaps I might sit in a particular spot when stopping the drama or engaging in discussion. I can stay in role until I need to draw the class together in order to examine the possible directions the drama may take. I may adopt more than one role during a lesson in order to satisfy the needs of the drama, choosing from a variety of roles depending on what I want to accomplish. The use of role may not always be appropriate: I may want to use another technique and then return to the use of role at another time. However, I need to transmit signals that indicate full belief in the role I am playing and in the dramatic situation. When working in role, I can open up a number of routes for enriching the drama: I can extend the drama from within the drama process; I can challenge the class in ways not possible as teacher, by being aggressive, supporting a minority view, moving the drama along or suggesting alternatives. Within the drama, I can elevate the language, supporting the contributions of the children, standing in the way of silly solutions or slowing down the action of the drama for clarification.

When I work in role to build a fictional world, I alter my status in the classroom. Children can then communicate with me and with each other in ways very different from those in real life in the classroom setting. I, of course, still retain control of the classroom, but the drama and the roles determine the direction of the work. If I play the role of an advisor to the king, who is in turn played by a child, then it is the child as king who will decide on the fate of the village. This altering of the dynamic of the interaction between teacher and child — the tone, the register, the choice of words, the implication of the speech — can give great freedom and strength to the voices of the children, and can present me as the teacher with opportunities for extending the type of talk in which children engage.

Working in role with the whole class also serves a very practical purpose; it allows me to guide inexperienced students in using the artform of drama, and then they can apply this learning when they work in small groups.

If I need to focus the class's attention I can be an old, wise elder, reminding them of the past; if I need to energize the group, I can present new information from across the mountain that endangers their prosperity; if I need to quieten them down, I can ask them in role to come one by one to me as the scribe of the village to record their deepest questions. This teaching repertoire allows me to operate in a useful frame with a group of children, and by carefully selecting the role I will find most useful, I can move the drama forward with increasing speed and significance. It also means that the children will have opportunities for making responses and for determining the relationships with the whole group. I find that when I'm going to roleplay with the children, I keep in the back of my mind six basic categories:

1. *Teacher as narrator.* This is such a useful strategy, for I can do so many things by simply saying, "I remember when." I can introduce my own personal memories to achieve empathy or to deepen the drama, or to tell a story about an unusual event that the children may face in future. I can summarize what they've done by referring to actual details that used in their drama, elevating their work by making it seem very special. I can close my eyes and jump time — decades or centuries, either backwards or forwards. As narrator or storyteller, I can consolidate the work, point toward new directions, reflect on what we've accomplished, or simply make the children feel good about their hard work.
2. *A leadership role.* Playing an authority figure such as a king, a boss or a mayor is a very powerful way to focus the drama

work and to give the children something to bounce against. If I don't know the class, I can quickly set up a tense moment or create a conflict by working as the one in charge. It does limit the opportunity for the children to be in control, so I tend to use this role at the beginning of a lesson to set up the situation, or at the end as a way of having children present their ideas. For me, it only works if the children have the power to make decisions or resolve conflicts. It is a thrilling thing to watch a child of seven battle a teacher in role as king, and come to persuade that king that what he has done is wrong.

3. *The opposer.* By playing the one who casts disbelief, who demands proof of status or simply opposes the one in charge, I can force the group to come together in opposition to the one in power. I may be the instigator, the one who forces the children to defend their decision, or who attacks their respect or dignity, forcing them to deepen their commitment. The role of the "devil's advocate" or the challenger is useful, but must always be framed in such a way that the children, through their diligent work, can argue against this interloper and come to better and stronger decisions.

4. *The lowest-status role.* When the children maintain the authority or high-status roles, I'm able to offer them a very different experience from the conventional role of the teacher, and it is most useful for working inside the group, as one of the crowd, a villager, a member of the crew, a servant. It distances me from the one in charge and the responsibility is shared among the group. If I am the one in the village who asks for help, then the status of the children is raised far above their actual position as students. This shift in power relation can be the most potent dynamic that results from the teacher working in role.

5. *The messenger.* In working in what we might call the intermediary role — the consultant, the one who asks for information, the reporter, the policeman — I can act as a link between those in the class with authority and those with low status. I'm able to focus the children and to pass on information, and yet not have to make a decision about what happens next. I'm simply framing the children's responses. This is a comfortable role for those of us not used to roleplaying.

6. *The shadow role.* It's not an actual role but most useful, as

described by Dorothy Heathcote. The teacher is inside the drama, assisting the children and structuring the work from a very indirect, non-specific role, such as a villager like everybody else, or a member of the community. But the teacher represents a committed and dedicated roleplayer. In truth, this is much like side-coaching in a traditional drama class, where we are able to gently help the children to focus and frame their ideas. This shadow role of course can merge into any of the other categories I've mentioned, such as a teacher working in a lower-status role, a teacher bringing information, or a teacher reflecting back to the children stories from past experiences with similar conflicts.

By adopting one of the lesser authoritarian models, teachers afraid to work in role can begin to feel the plethora of choices when working with a class of children. Suddenly you're not only asking questions, but asking them in a voice to which the children can respond with as much belief and feeling as possible. It is a way of modeling how to work in role without preaching. It is simply the most useful strategy in my teaching repertoire. And it is important to remember that in an ordinary lesson I will play two or three roles, depending upon the needs of the group at the moment; I have never maintained a role for a whole lesson. It's not necessary. There are so many ways I want to work with an individual child or a group of children that confining myself to one role limits possibilities. I want to instigate the drama, but then work with the group as a villager or in a shadow role, encouraging and supporting what the children are beginning to develop. I want to be teacher at times, calling them to come together and to share what we've done so far, where we should go next. Sometimes I sit in a particular place in the room so the children know that that is where the teacher resides and when in role I move to other places in the room. It is very humbling to have a child direct the drama rather having to do it constantly as the authoritarian teacher. When the one in charge of the action is the one who has organized and ordered the drama, and when that one is a child or a group of children, the teacher can observe the class in action, with opportunities to notice from the inside how the children are interacting. It is as if in reading we were suddenly inside the child's head, listening and watching as he/she becomes part of that story. The essence of roleplay lies in adopting a way of thinking, getting inside a character's life, imagining how you would behave if you were that person responding to the conditions and the tensions of the drama.

## MANAGING THE DRAMA PLAYERS

"The Golden Swans" is a folktale which has been told for generations in Thailand. The author of the version I know, Kermit Krueger, became interested in Thai culture in two years he spent as a Peace Corps volunteer in the area. The story comes from Chaiyapum province, on the mountainous western edge of the Mekhong plateau in northeastern Thailand. Because it is hard to reach, few people have ever seen the statue by the lake. Today, the people say that a century ago, after a terrible fire in the village, the inhabitants became golden swans that were allowed to visit the lake once a year. A stranger, unaware of the story of the swans, caught one and it died; the others fled and never returned. The local people captured the intruder, and his punishment was to spend his life creating a huge replica of a swan.

What does "The Golden Swan" have to say to thirty fifteen-year-olds in an inner-city school during a drama lesson? Perhaps the most interesting technique I tried involved the students' moving like birds. There was no flapping of wings, no weak bird calls, no trying to outdo each other. Each boy and girl felt the swan movement in their spines. Music helped. It was interesting to see Floyd, a seventeen-year-old Canadian native boy with no front teeth, the obvious class leader, becoming a part of the whole class, even when he was the swan statue. How did he feel that bird and show its flight while frozen? What made him experience a moment of real feeling at the telling of "The Golden Swans"? That is the magic of drama, and anyone can come under its spell.

## UNDER THE TABLE

For me, it is impossible to understand drama's effect on each child at all times. The development of language and thought is an ongoing process, and patience is required if we are to look for development in these areas. I was working with a class of grade six children in a school library, and when they entered, one child immediately lay down under a table in a remote spot in the room. Not knowing the children well, I decided to move into drama without him. I began with the book *The Trouble With Mr. Harris*, a story concerning fair play that examines both sides of an issue. I wanted the children to explore the responsibilities of the employee, the employer and the public. I read the book to the class, stopping at the point of a town meeting, and the loneliness of Mr. Harris as he was shown outside the town hall triggered the drama. The class created the town meeting "in the present moment." Volunteers described the unfair actions of Mr. Harris, the postmaster, being careful to depict them so that they could be seen from two viewpoints — that of the customer and that of the postmaster. The children told of packages damaged in the mail, of small children being told to play outside, of the post office closing on time even though there were customers waiting. There was a common sense of injustice as the frustration of the children and their roles combined in the cause of fair play.

The crowd agreed that the postmaster must be fired. The mayor was played by Rick, a class leader; I as teacher in role was Mr. Harris. The mayor asked Mr. Harris to come to a meeting for an announcement. However, I requested a chance to speak to the townspeople before the mayor's verdict was announced. I apologized to the townspeople and asked their forgiveness. Rick as the mayor was startled by this turn of events. He had been prepared to fire Mr. Harris. Now, in his role as mayor, he had to rethink the problem for several minutes. Finally he stated, "The postmaster will be given three weeks to shape up."

Everyone appeared satisfied with this solution. However, in discussion out of role, the class decided that Mr. Harris would be accused once more of being unkind. They developed a complex scenario involving a child's spicy words painted on the post office, Mr. Harris's reprimanding him and the child's accusation that he had been struck by the postmaster in anger. Once again in role, the class held a town meeting at which Mr. Harris was charged with the incident. Eventually he was found innocent and the mayor announced that he could stay on.

The class had shifted attitudes. They had moved from a quick decision to fire Mr. Harris to an appreciation of his unexpected change in motive and behavior. However, I wanted the class to understand the effect of their actions on Mr. Harris's future, to step back from a simple solution. In role, I refused the position of postmaster. I said I could no longer work for people who had no trust in me. As I turned to leave the room, the student lying under the table called out, ''We gave you three weeks — you give us three weeks! We'll prove that we trust you.'' I am always shocked at the complexity of the listeners, always surprised by the one who plunges deepest into the story pool.

# 7

## *Wolf Children I Have Known*
### (Drama Talk)

### EDUCATING THE WOLF CHILD

For several hundred years, cases have been reported of children who have been reared in the wild by animals, or kept isolated from all social contact. Sometimes the information is based on little more than a brief press report. At other times, the cases have been studied in detail — in particular, the stories of Victor, Kaspar Hauser, Amala and Kamala, and Genie.

During one summer session, I invited a grade four class identified as having behavioral problems to participate in our program. I chose a new story to work with, Jane Yolen's *Children of the Wolf*. The students sat on a rug in front of me and the teachers in a semi-circle behind them. I began with a discussion of books and films they had read, seen or heard about, concerning children raised by creatures of the jungle or the forest. The class recalled Tarzan, Mowgli and a wolf child remembered from rumor. I then presented the students with the problem to be solved through drama: "We are a group of scientists who have been awarded the contract for developing a program for humanizing a twelve-year-old boy, discovered living in a jungle, raised by wolves. In four years, it is our job to create a civilized sixteen-year-old man who will have a chance at a normal life. The first step for our group is to create a set of priorities concerning the training of the wolf boy."

Working in small groups in role as scientists, the children considered the various problems that confronted them in changing the feral child's behavior and inculcating values. Different groups developed strategies for working on the wolf boy's language, clothing, food, education, social habits and emotional needs. The small groups then presented their ideas to the whole class who, along with me in a neutral role as director of the project, questioned them and offered suggestions. The children were building a belief in the existence of the wolf boy, and as the members of each group processed the contributions of the class and altered their plans, they were using "talk in role" as their medium for learning.

I telescoped time by announcing that one year had passed, and each group must reveal the progress they had made with the wolf boy. The language of the children dramatically changed as the groups presented their findings. They took their roles as scientists very seriously, using their notes from their clipboards as the basis for their discussion. Their body language, choice of words, sense of audience, strength in role became much more complex. They seemed to think of themselves as authorities, as their commitment to the drama grew.

Later still, when presenting their findings at the end of year three, the first group announced that they felt the boy should be freed to return home. Their proclamation divided the class and we separated into two large groups, representing the opposing sides of the issue. The emotions were strong, resulting in a third group who were undecided and stood between the other two. The arguing continued, and those in the middle found themselves joining whoever was speaking at the moment.

Unfortunately, the school bus arrived and there was no completion to the drama, but the teacher had the children write me letters describing their feelings, and the following excerpts represent the range of opinions that grew from the work.

> I think he should be a boy.

> It was confusing to decide if he should be a boy or a wolf. It was hard I think that he should be a wolf.

> I like the story about the wolf-boy and I said the wolf-boy should have cooked food and the scientists said the wolf-boy should be in a white room to be studied and see how to eat the raw meat.

Thank you for inviting us to hear the story about the wolf-boy. We had fun with the scientists. I think we should leave him a wolf boy because he don't see no one to tell him something about people.

It was a very interesting morning. I enjoyed myself alot. It was real exciting. I also learned a great deal. It was a great experience for me and I will never forget that day.

And let the wolf boy do his own choice.

The children and I never saw the wolf boy or had anyone try to play him in role: there seemed no need for his presence. The class talked about him and created him in his absence. They cared passionately about his past, and argued with conviction about his future. Their language grew with the situation and with their belief in the wolf child. In role they were scientists who had begun to wear the mantle of the expert; they controlled the direction of the drama and the quality of the language; they had ownership of their work.

## WHEN CHILDREN CONTROL THE KNOWLEDGE

I chose the same beginning structure with a grade eight gifted class. I shared the cover of Jane Yolen's novel and we settled on the central questions of the drama, "What is the boy, wolf or human? What makes us human?"

Once again, I presented the problem: they had to civilize the wolf boy in four years and at the end of each year I asked for a report. In each report groups of anthropologists, sociologists and others had to discuss possibilities, organize priorities, synthesize opinions and finally stand and give an oral summary. Based on what they reported, I required a little more: if the wolf boy were given a pet by the scientists and got along with the pet, I asked that they try him with humans. If he was using a toilet but soiling his bedding once in a while, I asked that this problem be solved by the next year. At the end of the third year the boy was to appear on national television. The scientists announced that they were apprehensive because the wolf boy was still unpredictable. I suggested that they drug the boy for the appearance and they agreed. When one student questioned this method, I quickly said they must do this if the boy was to appear on television. I was testing to see if the moral issue would be picked up by the group, but it was not. The group of scientists did not come to the aid of the one student-scientist who had complained. But I knew the issue could be picked up later during reflection on the drama, so we carried on.

Finally, the wolf boy was ready. He was "human" according to the scientists and could appear on national television, communicating in an intelligent way with other human beings. After this the scientists had a sense of accomplishment and it was time to re-introduce the question that began the drama. At the end of four years, the boy's wildness was apparently gone and he was ready to join human society.

I chose to roleplay the wolf boy who was now, in appearance and behavior, a civilized human being. I asked to be returned to my "home," the wolf pack. The students in the role of scientists had to rethink their answers to the original questions, "What makes us human?" "What makes a wolf?" They had worked confidently for their "project leader," by using their knowledge of social sciences to civilize the wolf boy, and now he was saying to them, with the very words they had given him, "I want to go home." I asked those who would help me to step forward. I then turned to each of those who would not help and asked why they would not assist me in returning to my home. At this point the drama was at its most intense. Some children individually faced the wolf boy and began to realize the significance of their decision, whether it was to return him to the pack or keep him in human society. It became a lesson where the power of the work touched each participant, and what the children felt was depicted in their words, their faces and their actions.

Demands, especially of a technical kind, can elevate the situation. In this lesson, the children were "specialists" and used technical language befitting their roles. I acted as a manager to whom they must explain the situation, elevating their language in order to help them explain their success. The emphasis was not on the accuracy of the vocabulary but on the general tone with which the children spoke. Their expert roles were enhanced because they had to explain to someone less knowledgeable than themselves about their contribution to the program. Thus, the type of language demanded was always within their grasp. By controlling the knowledge, they had learned not only about the drama but about the power of talk itself.

Often, children in school are not given the time to hypothesize, to talk themselves into understanding, to "think aloud." Douglas Barnes calls this groping towards meaning "exploratory talk." It is usually marked by frequent hesitation, rephrasing, false starts and changes in direction. This type of exploratory talk is one means by which the assimilation and accommodation of new knowledge and old is carried out. Talking to learn must be part of every language interaction that is to have impact upon children. Talk can help children make sense "out loud" as they come to grips with new ideas and understanding. It is a bridge that helps them explore relationships that arise between what they know and what they are coming to know. When we are dealing with new ideas or coming to new understandings, our talk helps us make sense of both our thoughts and our feelings. If we can put our knowledge into words, then we begin to be able to reflect on that knowledge, to act on it and to change it.

Language is the heart of the drama process and the means through which the drama is realized. Drama may be the most appropriate means of providing the types of speaking/listening situations that good teaching now demands from teachers. It can facilitate a wide variety of language uses in contexts that require full participation within an affective/cognitive frame, promoting types of talk important in encouraging deep-level thought processes, such as expatiation, negotiation, clarification, explanation, persuasion and prediction.

In using drama as a teaching strategy, I need to create an environment in which talk is normal and desired, and in which the contributions of the children are valued not only by the teacher but by the other children. Because drama provides role situations different from those in regular classroom settings, children can begin to regulate the action. This will markedly affect the language use of everyone in the classroom, including the teacher. Modes, registers and qualities of language can be released more effectively through drama than in many other classroom situations. Both the children's confidence and competence in their languaging abilities are enriched and increased through the synthesis of language, feeling and thought.

While drama is an active, "doing" medium, reflecting on what happened presents a powerful way for children to make meaning by examining and understanding their thoughts and perceptions, both as spectators and as participants.

We want the children to ponder and consider the implications of what is happening within the drama. Dorothy Heathcote says they need to "stumble upon authenticity in their work" and to both experience and reflect upon their experience. Whatever techniques the teacher uses to promote reflection, they must not interfere with the drama as perceived by the children. The teacher can reframe the drama, freeze the moment, change the time, introduce new roles. It is after the drama that reflective discussion concerning the experiences and feelings that emerged provides opportunities for children to revisit and rethink their thoughts and observations about the issues and concerns raised in the drama. Children begin to think aloud, to grapple with the language they need to express their evolving ideas, to clarify and change their opinions. They begin to explain the motives and behavior evidenced during the drama, finding reasons and implications for assumptions and decisions they made. The thought and language that occur after the drama may be as important as the learning that happened during the development of the drama. The children, discussing collaboratively as a whole class, in small groups or writing in personal journals, look back on what they have done. They reflect as the teacher questions and deepens their ideas, giving them opportunities to make explicit the learning that occurred. (Sometimes children will be so involved with the drama that they find themselves discussing what happened in the drama while remaining in role.)

I enjoy reading the letters that classes send me, and their perceptions often alter my own understanding of what happened in the drama work itself.

Dear Mr. Booth,

I really enjoyed talking about the wolf boy. (Even if I pretty well knew or thought it wasn't true.) It was a very interesting subject. Although I am a shy person, I didn't talk much but enjoyed listening to others while having a bunch of thoughts whizzing through my head.

Jennifer

Of course, reflection may occur much later and be revealed informally in a seemingly unrelated context. This is what Gavin Bolton calls "analogous reflection," and occurs when children are able to relate principles that arose in the drama to other contexts. Teachers in their own classrooms have opportunities to observe these transferred learnings throughout the year.

I was visiting my brother Jack's grade eight class in June on the last day of school. After the children had been dismissed, a girl returned to the room, went to her desk at the back, walked over to us carrying an imaginary object and said in a soft voice to my brother, "I'd forgotten my mixing bowl from the village. Thank you." She had needed to tell her teacher of the importance of that lesson conducted in a long-ago January, when she had been allowed to be a woman in a tribe, a woman who had cast the vote determining if they would leave the area for a new home. The group did move on, and she had chosen to carry her bowl. Now she was giving it back to her teacher.

# 8

## *Are the Rumors True?*
### (The Role of the Storyteller)

WHEN CHILDREN TELL STORIES

Children have many stories to tell.
The issue is: Will they tell them to you?
                    Harold Rosen

"In most classrooms," writes Rosen, "the chief and privileged story-teller (of stories of any kind) is the teacher." Rosen's definition of narrative is broad, including personal anecdotes, recollections and experiences, in addition to more literary forms of story from the oral tradition such as folktale, myth and legend. His chief concern is with the story-creating process itself as a meaning-making strategy in the classroom.

Several years ago, I had the pleasure of listening to Bill Martin Jr. read aloud his story *The Ghost-Eye Tree* to a summer school of teachers. In the story, two children are afraid to walk past the ghost-eye tree in the middle of town, because of the stories told about its power. I knew then I had a perfect source for story drama, and I read the story to Craig Oliphant's grade four class at a demonstration session at a drama conference. The children and I shared personal anecdotes about frightening experiences; the participating teachers retold legends they had created previously to small groups of children, recounting the origins of the stories generated by the ghost-eye tree. Within the context of the ensuing drama, I, in role as a new teacher at the school, listened to the children roleplaying students volunteering to tell me the story of the village tree, and I questioned each aspect of their stories, causing them to elaborate and extend their legend through my seeming disbelief. When I chose to spend the night at the tree to prove the silliness of their stories, they attempted to dissuade me by sharing other incidents that had happened over the years to strengthen the tale of the tree's power, but I told them I was going to put an end once and for all to the rumors.

Out of role, the children discussed their feelings about the events that had occurred in the drama, and the following work was suggested by one girl who wondered how the children in the village would behave the next morning. This query demonstrates the storying that took place "inside the head" as she attempted to put together the elements of drama filtered through her own experiences.

The next scene was established by my entering the room as the principal, explaining that the teacher had not shown up for work and could not be reached at home. I asked the children for any information they might have about his absence, and none responded. I stopped the drama lesson at this point, told them my version of what I thought this lesson was about, and the class broke into groups in an attempt to explain the teacher's mysterious disappearance.

The whole class listened to each group's story, and after some discussion, accepted this as the official record:

> Mr. Booth went to the tree two years ago and fell and hit his head. Some people thought he was dead but really he has suffered some sort of memory loss.

Surprisingly, I received a package two years later from a student in Craig's class, explaining how her teacher had saved the subsequent writings of the children from my demonstration class and had used them inside a new drama with a different class. The storying continued for two years in the school setting, and, we hope, extends into their lives even now. I had been the original storyteller, but the children had gained the confidence to take over.

This drama work allowed children opportunities for telling stories of all kinds — recollections from the drama experiences as told by those who had lived through the fictional situation; personal anecdotes about what happened to the child both inside and outside the drama; personal stories stimulated by and enriched through the drama experience; literary retellings of the story used by the teacher to suggest the drama, retold from the perspective of the participants in role to those who must hear what has happened; collective stories by groups and by the whole class, wherein they revisited or recounted their own experiences drawn from the drama, in parallel to the teacher's story. Story-telling is a meaning-making process both within the drama and without, during reflective discussion and writing in private journals and in more public venues, such as group accounts for the classroom newspaper.

Rather than telling stories formally at the front of the class, I prefer that children begin building their narrative skills from inside the drama, retelling the story they have heard or read, and recounting anecdotes that relate to or grow from the drama, in role with the voice of the authentic storyteller.

In rereading my notes from the lessons in this book, I have come to realize that I retell, narrate, summarize and recount frequently in my work. My friend Bob Barton is a consummate storyteller, and I admire his ability to act as a medium for the hundreds of stories he has come to know, as he says, by heart rather than by memory. The continuum of storytelling incorporates a variety of styles, and drama has allowed me the strength in role to tell the stories I have read aloud for years, encapsulating what has gone before the drama, as I recount what happened in the story that the village hands down to its young, when I take on a role from a new point of view in an attempt to deepen or redirect the drama work. I can use story to slow down the actions, reminding the children of what has gone on, or preparing them for what may come next. Jonothan Neelands calls these "stories in action," developed from the responses of the group and the needs of the drama. We incorporate necessary details, elevate language, present a serious focus full of sub-textual significance and relate personal anecdotes from our own lives ("I remember when. . .").

Storytelling allows the children time to consider the dramatic activity they have been engaged in building. Rather than show their thoughts, they can tell them within the structure of story, in pairs, in small groups or as a large gathering. Brief narratives told by children in role can include gossip, rumor, wisdom, reports, observations, customs, culture, rules, codes, metaphors, examples. They can be told informally in small settings, or formally as an attempt to persuade the whole group of a particular point of view. Either way, they help children come to an understanding of what a storyteller needs to do to be effective in achieving his or her purpose — an invaluable lesson in creating learning experiences for children.

## WHERE DO STORIES HIDE?

When I am asked where I find my sources for drama I can only reply, "From everywhere." It is true that in my own work I use print sources as often as possible because I also am a literacy and literature teacher. Among thousands of childrens' books, naturally some speak to me louder than others as sources for dramatic exploration. In particular, the picture book is such an ingenious and all-encompassing source because so much can be discovered and rediscovered by the children as they explore both the language and the pictures. It's a unique medium because the words were written to be spoken and the pictures not to illustrate but to broaden and complement, so that the settings for these books are often rare and usually dramatic. The age of the children I work with seems to be irrelevant because I think that the picture book appeals to everyone, especially to today's visually oriented television viewers. The well-chosen picture book embodies those qualities of story and image that draw the children's own experiences to the page, and lets them see and hear new meanings as they negotiate between their own world and the world of the author/illustrator. The picture book can be the experience; drama can help make sense of that experience. Picture books open up opportunities for discussion and deepen understanding as the pictures draw the eye and the text catches the imagination.

Folktales are another source that allows me to use their bones as the beginnings of my drama work. If you think of them as preserved and performed by generations of storytellers, then they speak to the child in all of us, symbolizing deep feelings using fantastic figures and events. No matter how ancient a story is, it's not an archeological remain but a living tale that we can examine, offering glimpses of a particular time or a particular culture. These stories have acquired significance as they passed through time. Our stories of today are built on stories of the past.

The novel is a complicated source but it allows us to see just what story gives us as a framework. Since it is too long and complicated to be dramatized, the novel allows us to take from it themes that will act as supportive frameworks for our drama work. Children can combine an interest in the characters of the story and their own relationships with an inner exploration of themselves as they struggle to control the events in their own drama. As Bob Barton says, "instead of planning in a vacuum we start with a book that we know well and we find the power of drama within it."

### THE TALE TOLD IN ACTION

*The Red Lion* is a picture book by Dianne Wolkstein, and in a demonstration lesson with eight-year-olds and a group of teachers, I chose the role of a prince who was not supposed to speak to villagers. Therefore the children in role as my subjects had to go back and forth convincing the villagers, played by adults, that I should not have to follow a law that stated that I must kill a red lion in order to gain the power of a king, a concept taken from the story directly. A discussion was held with the children to gain ideas on how to persuade the villagers that the prince should be allowed to do what he believed and not follow tradition. In pairs, the children as ambassadors went off to the villagers, who were convinced that the red lion must be killed in the traditional way. The adults as villagers wanted to know why the prince was afraid and what he intended to do to gain power, and then explained that the prince must follow the rules of the land.

In role as the prince, I called my ambassadors together in order to find any new problems they might have considered with the villagers. A special badge of honor was issued to each ambassador and through this symbol, the power of the child's role was heightened. Before going forth to the villagers once again, a scroll was presented for them to carry to further enhance the sacredness of the mission. The scroll partially read, "... kill the lion within." As prince I sent my ambassadors out to explain what this meant to the villagers and any questions and doubts that the villagers had were brought back to the prince at the next meeting. With the students lying on their backs with their eyes closed, I narrated the story of how a mountain was climbed, and deep within a cave the scroll was discovered with this particular message addressed to whoever was in charge. The meaning of the scroll's message caused confusion among the children, but through questioning and discussion I was able to explore the concept of good vs. bad leadership as well as the ideas of loyalty, bravery and honesty.

One group of villagers asked if the prince had ever hated anyone or had been jealous of anyone. One child in the group explained that these emotions and others like them were the lion within: in order to use power for good one must destroy the evil or flaws in our characters. While this concept may have been difficult for the children to comprehend, what is significant is that through the drama they had an opportunity to learn as they stretched their intellects and strove for something slightly beyond their grasp. We had come a long way from killing a lion.

In another class where the scroll was not employed, the children decided to draft a letter to take to the villagers to explain the prince's refusal to fight a lion. They devised an elaborate scheme involving magic, chanting and the creation of a surrogate prince who was brought forth from a dream along with a surrogate lion. The wrestling of the lion and the prince, in slow motion, was a very powerful moment in the lives of those children, and somehow the demand for blood was satisfied by the use of the dream. And in truth, the lion in their story remained alive and the prince was not forced to kill it.

I want these types of stories, filled with power, where the ideas surge up from beneath the words. The books I use over and over are full of caves and shadows, subterranean tunnels, springs that bubble up in odd places, people who are never just what they seem, who trigger in us suspicion or surprise or sadness. I need stories that won't let go, that drag into their midst children who had no intention of entering, children who suddenly grasp the challenge, who at the very least try to escape from the red lion.

As a drama teacher, these are my stories, my tales and, ultimately, my dramas. And the tales the children create lie between the pages, revealing the imprint of the class every time I try to read the author's words.

# 9

## Living as a Knight Lived
### (Language Growth through Story Drama)

I was working with a group of children aged seven to ten from an alternative school in Toronto, and we were asked by their teacher to explore the theme "Knights of Old." I wanted them to begin to look at the significance of the word "knight." In *Harald and the Giant Knight* by Donald Carrick, a story set in medieval times, Harald and his family have had their farm taken over one spring by the baron's knights because the knights' regular practice fields have been flooded. They trample the farmer's crops and eat livestock, and Harald begins to reassess his concept of "knighthood." I chose to use in role a guest teacher, Tony Goode, visiting from England, so that more historical information could be fed into the drama to give the children material to "bump against." Earlier observation had told me that the children seemed to talk easily with a high degree of language competence. I began by reading the book to the class, stopping as I went along to examine the pictures with the children and to listen to their questions about the background of knights as presented in the story. We decided that the knights had held this spring training in the fields of local farmers, and that the farmers were very unhappy because considerable damage had been done. The farmers in medieval times did not hold title to the land and the lord of the manor collected rents in the form of produce.

In our first scene, the baron (our guest in role) met with tenant farmers who described damage done by the knights, and the farmers, in groups of three, created tableaux to show him the extent of the damage done. The baron pointed out that "the knights are mercenaries. Without them, we would all lose their protection. You must deal with them delicately."

The children resented the insensitivity of the knights. I asked them to roleplay the peasants collecting and hiding food to be eaten by the community before the knights destroyed the farm crops. While my role was very close to that of teacher/observer, I could still encourage imaginative language and begin to build in particulars of time and place. As the children mimed their offerings, I was able to notice them individually and began to use the space in the room to give them a sense of place. In role, we sat in a cave and demonstrated what supplies each had brought.

DB: Now we'll begin the drama. All of you are going to come to the cave to make your plans. Do you think we should go to the baron about our problems? What have you heard about the baron?

*Teacher Instruction*

*(General comments about the baron's power.)*

*Discussion In Role*

STUDENT: He owns all the land and we pay him rent and he never seems satisfied.

*Describing and Giving Information*

DB: I've heard rumors about other times it seemed to be his fault that people in the village died.

*Extending*

STUDENT: Could the baron stop us from picking wild blueberries to live on?

*Clarifying*

STUDENT: Anyway, we can't keep on living in caves and we can't live on his land in our cottages anymore.

*Focusing*

STUDENT: How can we live in these caves when the food is all gone?

*Supporting Previous Statement*

DB: Do you think if we all went to see him he would kill us all?

*Teacher Structure*

STUDENT: Could we sneak in or send a spy?

*Problem-Solving*

DB: We could send a child — he wouldn't hurt a child.

*Speculating*

| | |
|---|---|
| *(Some discussion about dressing up like knights or wearing disguises, and other alternatives that were rejected by the class.)* | General Discussion In and Out of Role |
| STUDENT: Why don't we just kill him and get rid of him? | *Suggesting* |
| STUDENT: His men would just kill us, you stupid. | *Arguing* |
| DB: Well, let's go watch him and see how he acts. Maybe there will be a chance to talk to him. Be careful not to threaten him — try to keep your tempers under control. | *Teacher Structure* |
| BARON: That's right! Get him while he's down! And who might you be? | *Second Teacher In Role* |
| CHILDREN: We're farmpeople. We are just looking at the jousting tournament. | *Describing* |
| BARON: Well, be sure and keep out of the way. | *Adding Tension* |
| BARON: Watch out, there, Sir Daigle... What are you people staring at me for? | *Confronting* |
| DB: It's just that we have never seen knights on our farms before. | *Clarifying* |
| STUDENT: Yeah, they ruined them. | *Criticizing* |
| STUDENT: They chopped down all of our fruit trees and stole our food. | *Informing* |
| BARON: Well, you're not blaming my knights, are you? | *Confronting* |
| CHILDREN: Yes we are. | *Showing Commitment* |

By having Tony Goode, with his British dialect, as a guest in role the children were taken into a situation where the roles had immediate differences in status. At first, this resulted in some laughter, but before long the children were inside the drama because of Tony's strength as a teacher and belief in his role. Their own language began to reflect their degree of commitment, and as they moved in and out of belief, their language power fluctuated. The original story seemed far away at the end of the lesson, but in retelling it at the conclusion of the drama, the details fell into place.

In story drama, children are building their own story inside the drama, and in this case, the concept of "knight" was explored in a very different manner from that of the book. I felt it important to help the children build a bigger frame for the word, and

I had to work in role along with them to refocus the drama when they were not able to see the consequences of their actions. It was important that they explore the position of the baron and the reason behind the killing. Many of my tentative suggestions were rejected. I had to push very hard to slow down the acceptance of the knight by the villagers so that the children could begin to put the whole picture of this society together. In discussion away from the baron and knight, the language was very informal and the role commitment minimal. We required the theatrical tension of the baron or knight to stimulate the thought/language response. Of course, not all children were using powerful language constantly, but there were times when they were all involved, listening and observing in an emotionally connected mode. Later on in the improvisation, the villagers agreed to take an oath, and those moments were very intense. While the children were only repeating phrases given by the teacher, their commitment to their roles was evident and their belief was revealed in the quality of their language: the words became their own.

As a teacher, it is my constant obligation to let the children begin initiating the drama and the language play as soon as possible, and to know when to withdraw and when to intervene. In story drama, language can be one of the best indicators of learning, with regard to both story comprehension and the effect of drama. The following letters and diary entry show how rich the language and ideas can be.

Your Highness,

Your knights have to get off our farm. We have to grow our crops because we need to give crops to the baron. They are cutting down all the trees.

Your servant
David R.

Your Royal Highness,

I have a very big problem and I would like you to help us stop it. The problem is that our crops are getting trampled over by the knights. Please help us. They are stepping all over our fields on their horses. Thank you.

From your loyal fruit farmer, Amanda.

Today I summoned the knights of the round table, for a special reason. I had a difficult task for the bravest ones in the land. Indeed they were brave, even blowing out a candle in the darkest land. The knights taught me a special lesson. It was a gift of love. It was hard for me to understand at first this gift of love. They presented me with ways of saying what love is. They brought me a rose of the colour red, when they came to me with the rose I didn't want to take it but it was so beautiful that I couldn't resist. Then I received a blue rose and explained that the red rose represented love and the blue hatred. Then came a kitten but I refused. I said I had a cat and I didn't want a white kitten I said my black cat was my companion. So I left but came back without being called. I had lost my cat and I knew that they meant to hurt it and now they had it. The knights said that I loved my cat and that's why I cared about it so much that I felt sad. We made a promise I would not hurt their loved ones if they gave me my cat, so they did. I am writing from my spell chamber, and if anyone ever reads this diary, I put in a message to all fellow sorcerers. It is as follows: The gift of love is a beautiful thing. If you learn to love you can easily live with it.

Marion

### DID YOU HEAR WHAT YOU SAID?

In drama, the children are allowed to talk themselves into believing in the fiction, to hear their ideas bounced back, to reframe and refocus their own information and attitudes, to recognize the need for communicating what they believe to those who believe differently, to actually hear language at work. Their words sweep them into thought, and as they recognize the truth of what they are saying, that very language is transformed into new patterns. It determines the action and lets them see the impact, all while they are in the midst of the action, in the eye of the hurricane.

The learning in drama occurs with the experience of being involved directly, so that the students think on their feet as participants. As a teacher, I must move the students into areas of significance where they will be challenged to learn. I cannot detract from their part in shaping the drama, but rather must build upon it. I can handle decisions concerning styles, strategies and activities, informed by an understanding of the students' needs in a particular situation.

I try to direct their attention not just to the subject of the discussion, but to the very language they are using in the drama. As well, I can alter the mode of communication, letting the students argue, inquire, persuade, inform, explain, discuss and reflect. The deeper the drama, the better the potential for language development. I can help children by structuring and limiting the decisions to be made in the drama lesson and by opening the range of options available to them in coping with the situation.

When I become a member of the ensemble, in role, I am able to alter control of the communication systems in the classroom. Alternative communication patterns are set up in the dynamics of a drama situation where the right to control talk is determined by the context of the drama, rather than by socially ascribed roles, such as that of the teacher as regulator and instructor.

The children gain new understanding about what language is suitable in a particular context. I then have a powerful technique to help them reshape their own knowledge. They can begin to take responsibility for their own learning, influencing the events that occur. The children and I begin to negotiate our relationships within the drama framework. They begin to spontaneously elaborate on the situation, contributing language and exploring alternate language functions. The initiative to communicate is in the hands of the children, and they have some decision-making power concerning what language is appropriate.

FROM PRETENDING TO BELIEVING

The impact of language on drama was made evident to me while working with a hundred and fifty grade seven to grade thirteen drama students and forty teachers participating in a series of drama workshops. My contribution involved a session with the whole group in the afternoon in a play-making session that was to highlight a local sesquicentennial celebration theme. In planning my structure for the work, I realized I could not simply tell the group that they should care about their history. They would have to appreciate the past inside the drama frame. After introducing the theme, I divided the participants into small groups and had them prepare various aspects of it, using different strategies such as choral speaking, movement, music and set design. Later, the groups came together in an ensemble improvisation.

The visual arts group, using tin foil, plastic sheets and lights, had changed the meeting room into a futuristic holding tank. As the other students entered the transformed space, they were in the setting for the drama. In role, I explained that they were to be held prisoner here until all vestiges of national history had been "wiped from the slate," so that the society of the future would hold no prejudices or past allegiances, and we could begin to build a new and totally free nation. As the drama work grew, it was the language that changed most drastically. One student's summary describes her perceptions of the experience.

> "No! Not the treatment!" cried one of the bolder prisoners in mock terror. Such idle threats could not intimidate us. Instantly the merciless jail warden spotted his prey and silenced him with one fell swoop of crossexamination. Some were overpowered by his strength, but others stood their ground. Our heritage was on trial.
>
> I had the privilege of being a prisoner for an afternoon. . .
>
> The atmosphere was so intense and unified that we burst into singing, an effort to overwhelm the judge. The improvisation ended nicely when two prisoners stood up and led us in the singing of "O Canada" in role. For once the anthem meant much more to me than a minute and a half of regulated morning exercises. It was a satisfying conclusion to a fun and interesting day of creative sharing.

The student had seen herself and others shift attitudes, and the quality of the language was the indicator. She begins her account by stating that the comments at the beginning of the lesson were made in "mock terror," and I concur. The older students required much more time to accept the artifice of the situation and to suspend disbelief. But as the action moved on, the tone, the syntax, the volume of the comments began to alter. The participants' arguments deepened as their language strengthened, driven by the emotion of the moment. The students resented and resisted the implication that history was of no importance. As I in role hammered at the elimination of all history, they in turn fought passionately against me in their defence of keeping what they felt was theirs. And they prevailed in the end: I concluded the drama after they sang "O Canada."

The participants had moved to using the words of others, the lyrics of an anthem, as support for their struggle. But they had made those words their own.

# 10

## When the Buffalo Are Gone
### (Encouraging and Promoting Thinking)

WHERE WILL WE HIDE THE BUFFALO?

The drama lesson involved a group of grade four, five and six children from a summer school in the arts who had volunteered to work with our teachers on a drama course. In a dramatic situation in role as a tribe of North American native people, they had to make a decision about sharing their few remaining buffalo with a neighboring tribe. The source for this drama was *The Iron Horse* by Paul Gobie. After reading the story to the children, I asked them to imagine a time when the Plains Indians had lost entire herds of buffalo to white hunters who seemed unaware of the buffalo's importance to native people. To these marksmen, the shooting of herds of buffalo from the windows of trains was mere sport.

The teachers on course and the visiting children became the buffalo, and while I kept a beat on the tambourine, the buffalo grazed quietly, until the sound of approaching danger sent them stampeding. The group ran in place, creating a thundering sound. Then I used the tambourine as the sound of a rifle, and the older buffalo were shot one by one until none remained alive. While the adults remained motionless on the floor, I went around and discussed with the children how the native people might have felt about this slaughter, when their lives depended on an abundance of buffalo. The children were concerned that the settlers had killed the creatures so wastefully, while the native people had considered them sacred. Now in role as native people, the children decided to round up the remaining buffalo and hide them so that the animals would not starve or freeze in the winter.

I began to narrate:

Nobody knows this but us. And we know where the buffalo are, and we have them hidden. There might be another tribe that needs food, and that's who this group of adults will become. They're another tribe of Indians on the prairies. Their buffalo have all been killed by the white hunters and they want animals to start their stock with. If we give up our hundred buffalo, we will not have enough to start our own stock . . .

We then divided into two tribes: those who had lost their buffalo (the adults) and the tribe whose buffalo were kept hidden (the children). In the drama, the adults had to convince the children to share their buffalo. As teacher-as-narrator, I had introduced the context for the drama with a built-in problem/conflict: ("Why would they want our buffalo? We need the hundred buffalo for self-sufficiency.") In her journal a child commented later on the dilemma.

I think that we should not trust the other tribe and not help them because when it was the buffalo hunting season the other tribe did not hunt for food but we did. Now they want us to give them our food. Yet if we have enough food we should help them out. The reason I think we can't help them is because we don't have enough buffalo for both our tribes. If that is the question — which tribe would survive — I think it would be the tribe that set out hunting for buffalo before winter season. It is also hard to see the other tribe die but if we could help them we would. Although if we hunt other things and join forces we could hunt more and faster.

I intervened to clarify the problem, questioning the children about possible solutions. The girls of the tribe with the buffalo wanted to take food to the hungry and medicine to the sick of the other tribe, but were persuaded by the boys not to sacrifice the buffalo, or their herd would dwindle. Instead, they shared what little corn their own families had. The boys didn't trust the other tribe, and were angry that their food was being shared. However, I revealed that the women alone possessed the secret of where the buffalo were hidden, and had refused to tell it to the men.

The leaders of the buffalo people were sent back and forth to negotiate with the other group, but in the end they continued to insist that their tribe alone needed the hidden buffalo to survive.

As the class period ended, the children had still not solved the problem, and out of role, I summed up the drama: "This is a story about a tribe who had the wisdom to maintain their buffalo stock for their children's children. It is the story of a tribe whose women took food from their own children's mouths to help others in need. It is the story of a tribe who had a treasure burden. Your treasure is your future, and you are burdened with it."

> In all of this it is important to note that David allowed the drama to evolve from student responses so that the story was theirs. (The students decided on the dance interpretation and the girl decided to share her food.) It was only on one occasion when he "shaped" the drama by maintaining that the hidden buffalo were still there and this input was essential for the drama to proceed.
>
> His input as tribesman was interesting when he acted as challenger to the girls who had shared their food. ("You gave them half the food; now there is only enough for one family. You are endangering your tribe.") He also challenged one girl, accusing her of being a "spy" and suggested the others may have betrayed the secret.
>
> This served several purposes. It immediately focused on responsibility and consequences of accepting a role. The implications of this role were immediately brought home to her and to those who rallied around her, thus serving to deepen their sense of belief, commitment and roleplay. It also intensified the drama by adding an additional inner conflict which forced students to move beyond an easy-ending solution to a complex problem.

During follow-up sessions with their teacher, Alistair Martin-Smith, the children continued to try to find a solution to their problem by setting out on a journey together with the other tribe, to find a place where they could hide the buffalo together so they would never be found by the settlers. During the journey, they learned to trust one another by sharing the difficulties which beset them. They painted maps of the journey so that they could one day find their way home, and they shared the stories they had written in their journals of how they received their Indian names.

The structure encouraged personal, verbal "immediate" reflection by a number of students. One girl made the parallel of buffalo killing with present-day duck-hunting. Another boy maintained that people killed for fun then because they had little to do in terms of entertainment (videos, etc.). A girl made a comparison with human frailty of the past and with the present condition for human error. Certainly, one of the questions each student must have asked was "What is our present-day connection with nature?" This was made clear when David pressed for information about cows and milking and it was obvious that few of them had any awareness of animals.

On a non-verbal reflective level, students were led to a consideration of loyalty (peers/group versus individual), to the motivations for killing (perhaps beyond hunting) and to a sense of what it feels like to struggle for survival in the face of technology (muskets). There could be an increased appreciation for the sense of the importance of life ("the tribe was wiped out — they are no more") and the nobility of indigenous peoples. It forces them to consider realistic choices one has to make in terms of survival. (Shall we live for the good and maintenance of "us" and does that involve negation of "them"?) Is there such a creature as a hero who could emerge from the drama and face our dilemma? Students can move from a consideration of the specific to universal themes and questions, thus deepening feeling/thought processes and broadening exploration.

## THINKING IN ROLE

Contemporary education is concerned with developing thinking processes in children. Every curricular guide embodies this principle in its goals; every teaching workshop is related in some way to techniques for aiding cognitive development in children. What implications does this have for drama teaching, so much of which has concerned the "feeling" side of the learning spectrum? Is there room for encouraging thinking, for demanding thinking, in a contemporary drama lesson? Can drama fit within the academic curriculum? Can drama be a basis for thoughtful learning?

Often the arts tend to be wholly associated with the affective domain, but the cognitive should be — has to be — part of any teaching.

As we have seen, inventiveness and problem-solving can be developed through gathering information, planning and selecting materials, describing artistic problems, modifying and examining materials and information, experimenting with alternatives and implementing solutions and sharing them with others. In this sense drama is both a subject matter and a teaching approach of inherent value to promoting thinking.

Learning is a process that begins with the known reality of the children. The teacher helps the learners move beyond, into unknown areas, developing hypotheses about issues and concerns that intrigue them, testing those hypotheses through problem-solving activity and reflecting about the consequences of their actions. By being part of the learning, by interacting and dialoguing, children come to understand the process of imaginative inquiry. They act upon and take responsibility for their own personal changes, and focus on human concerns, both as individuals and as members of society. Factual information, such as the death of the buffalo in the case cited earlier, becomes real to children through their involvement in the drama, as they participate in decisions and in events determined by them as they consider the consequences of their actions and the impact of the information on their own lives and the world in general.

It is the balancing of the two experiences at the same time that allows the children to make meaning, and it is this negotiated meaning that makes drama a learning opportunity. The children create new perceptions and understandings, modifying their existing concepts and attitudes from both outside and inside the experience and developing a subjective/objective relationship with the world. The children forge links with their real world and the world of illusion, making meaning, which is, after all, the goal of thought.

## WHO WILL ASK THE QUESTION?

In a typical story drama, I ask dozens of questions but I must ask them not as "teacher," but as the one who needs to know. This switch in the role of a questioner is very useful in drama for now I am able to ask a child a question to which I don't know the answer, to which there is no single, correct response. Instead

I am part of the drama, asking for the students' viewpoint and their interpretation of the ideas we've evolved so far. I want to be a teacher in drama who encourages and promotes the children's ideas, who acts as a catalyst in order to stimulate their minds or challenge their joking responses. I want to use my questions to help them think of new ways of entering different areas of the drama. I want the questions to be real, I want them to be authentic. As in a real conversation, we ask questions that need to be asked for clarification. If I list my questions on a paper before I begin, they never quite fit into the transitional work. If we think of the functions of questions, then perhaps we can as teachers find those questions that will help the children dig deeper into their work.

1. Information questions require the children to seek information and research from material such as books and documents, or from adults, or to supply information from their own experiences. We need to make specific decisions about where we go next. "Where does the tribe get its water supply?" "How many horses will we need for the journey?" "Where will we hide the buffalo we have found?" "How many days will it take us to reach the hiding place?"

2. We can ask questions that help the group locate where they are in space and time. "Show me where the other tribe was seen." "What place in the village do you live?" "Where do you stand when the leader comes into the village?"

3. There are questions that control the class: "How can we get past the guards so they won't hear us?" "Where can we sit so everybody can see?" "Which ideas shall we choose?" "Have you heard them all?" "Who will come forward and feed the hungry?"

4. There are questions that deepen insight or help children build belief in the situation: "What will we not be able to do now that the buffalo have disappeared?" "When the chief is away what will we miss about his ruling?" "Do the men in this tribe have any feelings?"

5. There are questions that offer alternatives or limit choice: "Who will stay behind to guard the herd?" "Will the girls be able to achieve what the boys have done?" "Will we escape?"

6. There are questions that imply action, that get the kids moving and doing: "Line up behind the leader." "Check the water for impurities." "Help move the rock away from the mouth of the cave."
7. There are questions, of course, that encourage reflection. "What sort of leader will we need?" "What will we want the leader to do for us?" "On this journey, where did we need stronger leadership?" "What other ways could we have dealt with the forces against us?"

Often the best question is simply a statement or a suggestion, because it motivates the children into responding. And of course, if you work in role, you have another thousand voices that can ask the question. Naturally, the most significant questions are asked by the children.

# 11

## Reading the Tiger Tracks
### (Literacy and Drama)

### ENTERING THE PRINT

I was working with a story in the children's reader, *The Dancing Tigers*, by Russell Hoban, a complex picture book that uses the folktale idiom to deal with the problem of modern society's encroachment on nature. In the story, a Rajah disturbs jungle life by bringing taped music along on a tiger safari, and in revenge, the tigers actually "dance the Rajah to death." How this occurs is suggested in the book, but when I asked the children how he had died, they were unable to tell me. They had not been able to make sense of this crucial element of the story.

Drama is a tool for unlocking meaning, and so I chose a role as the Rajah's son who had returned from America to discover the reason for his father's death. The children in role as trackers and servants gave me various explanations about his death, conjectured from their own knowledge, but unrelated to the story. Eventually, two students volunteered the information that the Rajah had been danced to death. In role, I angrily rejected their responses, claiming that I no longer accepted such superstitious beliefs since I had been educated in North America. It was now up to the students to prove the truth of the story to me, since I had ordered them locked up until they disclosed the real reasons for his death. Out of role, I worked with the students in groups as they set about planning to explain to the Rajah's son what had happened on that safari.

When we returned to role, the children demanded the opportunity to prove that the Rajah had indeed been killed by the dancing tigers. They asked the son to accompany them on a similar safari, where similar music would be played, and when this had been agreed to and the ensuing drama had begun, everyone was sitting with me in a circle. Then two children, as tigers, began the Dance of the Silence that is Partner to the Violence. As we watched, I was suddenly taken by both arms and told politely to leave the tigers or I would meet my father's fate. The children had understood the concept of the tale; by teaching me, they had unraveled the threads of information and come to grips with an experience outside their own frame of reference. They had made sense of the story by reliving it through drama. Thus, an elaboration of the story led to a more thorough examination of one of the story events. As the children took on the roles of the servants, they brought to the drama not only all they knew about the story situation but also all they knew about being questioned by authority, and all they knew about innocence and truth.

The children and I attempted to construct meaning from print through drama, in preparatory discussions in a drama setting of "people in a place with a problem to solve" (e.g., servants meeting in a hall to answer the questions of the Rajah's son); by working within different structures within the drama setting such as divided into pairs or subgroups with tasks (writing a petition to the Rajah's son or inventing a good explanation to satisfy him); by having the teacher take a pivotal role within the drama itself (e.g., that of the Rajah's son); by having the teacher take a neutral role which allows him or her to question or elicit responses within the drama (e.g., a child played the Rajah's scribe who came to record the answers to the teacher's questions); or by the children taking charge of the drama (e.g., they must help keep the tigers safe from outside elements).

*The Dancing Tigers* has served me well for a dozen years, and the Rajah's death has been explained to me so many times by young people who on first reading could make no meaning, but who, with the drama, fought for their lives with this previously unbelievable piece of information.

They were teaching us rats to read. The symbols under the picture were the letters R-A-T. But the idea did not become clear to me, nor to any of us, for quite a long time. Because, of course, we didn't know what reading was... as to what all this was for, none of us had any inkling.

Robert C. O'Brien,
*Mrs. Frisby and the Rats of Nimh*

No one "reads reading"; everyone reads for a purpose. Every word is a process, and the reader is as important a part of that process as the text. As in drama, the reading experience is a personal one: the reader understands what the words say to him or her, translates the experience he or she has read about into his or her own context, and responds with feelings and attitudes about the experience and the text. It is common for teachers to discuss the knowledge relevant to a text (awareness of the source, the author, traditions and techniques). However, not much time has been devoted to those qualities that the reader brings to the text (feelings, experiences, attitudes, values and beliefs).

The child's awareness of possible meanings and patterns is vital to that child's reception of language and to the production of language, and the child derives this awareness from hearing and using language. Educator James Moffett says that raw experiences and human socializing are the bases from which verbalization and literacy are derived. One does not need to be able to read and write in order to comprehend and compose language. Obviously both can be done orally, by preliterate or illiterate people. Meaning is a larger, lifelong matter, connected to literacy only because letters symbolize speech. Meanings are learned through one's total life experience and no more by reading instruction than in any other way. To derive full comprehension, a reader must become the co-author, absorbing the concepts presented and then scrutinizing and assessing those ideas in the light of his or her own knowledge and experience. What accounts for the understanding a reader is able to bring to bear on a book at any given moment are experiences between readings — warm-ups and follow-ups that help him or her to grasp a text better when alone with it. What is needed for good comprehension are strong motivation before reading and strong intellectual stimulation afterward. Answering comprehension questions usually affords neither, but drama may succeed.

There is a lack of specific information for teachers on drama in education's effect on the development of reading ability. The term "creative drama" usually appears in manuals used in reading series and in reading texts. However, the actual dramatic activity suggested is often an introduction to the reading selection, a follow-up activity or an outgrowth of the reading lesson. At best, drama is seen as peripheral to the reading program. What is meant by drama in such materials is not clear. Often the "drama" activity is simply a word game or a physical exercise to release tension. How drama influences the child's reading comprehension has seldom been examined. The true relationship between drama and reading is much deeper than just making the former an adjunct to the latter.

Children learn by testing hypotheses and evaluating feedback. Relevant feedback is any reaction that tells the child whether the hypothesis is justified or not. Children must comprehend what they are doing all the time they are learning. It is the possibility of making sense that stimulates them to learn. Many devices used in school to train the reader to note exact details in a text may result in producing a reader who, in making the effort to come more closely to grips with the exact meaning of an author, abandons the attempt to relate the significance of what he or she reads to his or her own social life. The teacher must, in helping children reveal their comprehension, be concerned with how and what children identify within their reading, with what they feel to be synonymous and analogous to their own lives and with their ability to see relationships. We must provide opportunities for the reader to realize that other child readers of the same text have found different ideas and understandings in it.

The relationship between the two learning areas of drama and reading lies in the world of meaning. It is the idea of symbolization and its role in the discovery and communication of meaning that connects drama and reading. Both areas are concerned with interaction. In story drama, the children enter into a dialogue, modifying and exploring symbols by changing and challenging each other's contributions. When reading, they enter at first into a dialogue with the author, then with other readers and finally with themselves. Through discussion and analysis, they modify and develop their understanding of the author's meaning, as well as absorbing the diversity of meanings their classmates have taken from the text. In both cases, children are negotiating at the symbolic level.

Whether the situation the drama is based upon is original or from literature is of little significance. The drama must elaborate on facts to find hidden truths and universal concepts, not just retell events from memory. Weak drama, like weak reading, is concerned with words rather than with the meanings behind them.

Going beyond the text requires that the teacher's techniques somehow relate the concepts in the text to the child's experiences. In this way, fundamental memories brought forth by the intensity of the reading or drama experience are tapped so that the resultant response is both personal and universal, and can be shared in the context of the literacy situation and the dramatic experience. Then the literary code will be broken and the context made significant to the "theory of the world" that each individual is in the process of creating as he or she is educated — in the widest sense of the word.

In my experience with *The Dancing Tigers*, what has happened is a wonderful synthesis of print and drama, each fulfilling in its own right, but unbelievably powerful when used together.

# 12

## Monsters I Have Created
### (Writing and Drama)

*Vodnik* is a Czechoslovakian folktale about a horrible creature of the lake who wanted to marry a mortal, Manya. Its central conflict is the heart of a story drama unit. What tales have people told about Vodnik? How did the stories begin, years ago? Why weren't the stories forgotten? These questions became the focus of our dramatic activity in a first grade setting.

Through group discussion and storytelling in role, each family in the class "village" made up the mythic origins of the creature. The stories were supposed to be told by the village members late in the evening, as volunteers from each group shared what they had created. In an attempt to draw tourists to the village, an imaginary museum was built, displaying these stories, and a photographer took publicity photos of the creations (tableaux were created in groups, and a child then took actual Polaroid photos). Signs were written to warn people of the dangers and to create interest in tourists. Each family allotted part of its home for tourist facilities and made advertisements for these facilities. The village planned a giant surprise party for Manya on her twenty-first birthday, since she had no family. A child volunteered to roleplay Manya, and each family brought a gift, a treasure from their own heritage, as well as contributing a special dish to the dinner. The villagers sat down at banquet tables in the town hall, and the gifts were presented to

Manya. Minimal props were used — most of the action was mimed. People passed around the food, and drinks were served. Then there was a knock at the door. When a child in role as mayor answered, in role as Vodnik I entered the hall and demanded to marry Manya, stating that I would return in one half-hour for the decision. When I had left, the mayor announced that the village would have to decide if Manya should be helped. There was much discussion in role, as the villagers feared for the safety of their children and for their own lives.

After the discussion, I presented Manya with the situation: if she volunteered to marry Vodnik, the village would be spared. After some hesitation, Manya offered to go with Vodnik. However, the village refused to allow this, and plans were hatched to save her from this fate. One family offered to hide her; another felt that if she appeared to have a terminal disease, Vodnik would leave; another decided to make a "Manya-balloon," filled with grenades which upon being touched would explode, killing Vodnik. Others attempted to build traps of various types. At length a plan was voted on and adopted: a large net would be placed on the ceiling of the town hall. Manya would stand in the middle of the room as bait. As Vodnik approached her, a signal would be given, Manya would dash to safety and the entire village would reach up, grab the net and pull it over the creature, thus trapping him. The plan was engaged.

As Vodnik, I knocked at the door. A volunteer answered, and I took her hand. This caused the crowd concern, since they realized two people were about to be trapped in the net — the volunteer as well as Vodnik. The boy who was to give the signal looked around in panic, unsure of when the net should be pulled. Suddenly the signal was given, and Manya ran from Vodnik. The volunteer who had answered the door pulled free and escaped. Vodnik was trapped, amid cheers from the villagers.

After the completion of this drama work, I read the entire book to the class. In their follow-up writing activities, carried out in the classroom under the direction of the teacher, the children were asked to speculate on Vodnik's origins. In the cases below, written by the students, one can see the specific impact of the drama on four different children.

Vodnik was a mean person. He kept people in jars. In the picture you will see Vodnik's weapons and him. The needle is for shrinking people so they can fit in to the jar and there is no way to get out of the jars.

By Maxeen

Once there was an ugly, slimy animal and his name was Vodnik. He is from the ocean and he was born in a shell and he goes up every night in to the village and one night he opened a door and there was Manya. He said, "I will marry you," and he went to the ocean where he lives and he said to Manya, "I will be back in five minutes," and Manya was scared and she did not know how she could get out of it. She went to the village and she said to a villager, "Can you keep me in your house?" And she did do that... The end.

Thank you,

Jana

Long ago there was a frog up in space. The space frog kicked the frog out of space and the frog fell into the lake. The frog sealed people's souls into glass jars. No one knows where they are.

Philip

Dear Mr. Booth,

I liked the play very, very much. Did you like the play too? What part did you like best? I do not know what part I liked the best. Thank you for inviting me to do the play with you. It was one of the best plays in the world. Thanks very much! Thanks for inviting the class too. I think the class liked the play very much and I think that they liked you very much too. Did you like the class too? I liked you. Did you like me too? We did a better story than the book did. Do you like the story that we did better or the story that the book told? Well?

From Caleb

The writers in these examples used the reflective composing time in unique ways, as they attempted to describe what had happened, investigated motivation for the actions of the characters or pondered the reasons for the results of the whole interactive process. The drama provided context for the writing, and the writing illuminated the drama work.

Educating the imagination is a difficult and complex task, and it is a slow developmental process as children work in the written mode. Drama can help give them skills in using processes that may transfer to writing.

Today's writing curricula stress the active use of writing rather than exercises about the act of writing. In some classrooms, traditional motivations for writing have not dealt with inner compulsion or need, but only with the completion of creative writing tasks. I have found that when writing is embedded in a context that has a personal significance for the writer, the writing skills themselves will be enhanced. If children are engaged in the expressive and reflective aspects of drama, living through "here and now" experiences that draw upon their own life meanings, then the writing that accompanies the drama and the writing that grows out of it may possess the same characteristics and qualities.

The process of writing can be a language form in which engaged writers/participants explore their feelings and ideas, learning not only to express themselves but to rethink, reassess, restructure and re-examine their work and perhaps even come to an understanding of the needs of the reader. The children begin to think of themselves as writers, controlling the medium in order to find a way to say what they want to say to people they want to reach. Writing in role or as a result of having been in role lets children enter a new sphere of attitudes and feelings. As they try for a more complex imaginative understanding of what is happening in drama, their writing generally becomes more complex and their language deepens. Because writing may be used within the drama and may be read or listened to by others, there is a built-in reason to proofread and edit.

Drama can act as a strong prewriting activity for anything from free writing, journals and letters to interviews, brainstorming, lists and so on. As well, it provides many opportunities for collective writing, in which groups collaborate on a mutual enterprise. For example, they can co-operate in collecting data, organizing information, revising and editing, all inside a context for learning.

Drama itself can involve written language in a variety of forms: letter writing in role; creating announcements, proclamations and petitions; reporting about events within the drama and in reflective journals; designing advertisements and brochures; inventing questionnaires and important documents; and writing narrative stories that are part of or that are conjured up by the drama.

The concrete contextual framework provided by dramatic situations can both encourage and enable students to compose and transcribe for authentic reasons. The discussions and reflections arising from the possibilities and explorations within imagined and felt situations can lead to a variety of written activities. As well, many of the conventions of drama can lead naturally to literary conventions:

- a town meeting can result in a transcript;
- a witness can create a monologue;
- an incident can become a piece of reporting.

Writing generated in response to the concrete particulars of context can be connected to real human situations, not only treated as classroom practice. The relationship of talk and writing is emphasized, with language experienced as a whole. We write to see what we think we have said.

# 13

## *Three Thousand Voices*

### (Reading Aloud in Drama)

A few years ago, I was asked to take part in the annual conference for the Michigan International Reading Association. However, rather than addressing the delegates, I was to work with the children of Detroit, since the committee felt that a conference devoted to reading should begin with an event dedicated to the children who might benefit from such an affair. It was decided that they should have a participatory reading experience followed by a performance by a circus: I was to conduct the former, and Ringling Brothers/Barnum and Bailey Circus would provide the latter. I hesitated to accept the offer, for although I had worked with thousands of children in dramatic activities, the sheer number of children — more than three thousand — was daunting. However, the challenge proved too intriguing, and I found myself in an open-air arena on the banks of the Detroit River with thousands of children in front of me and a microphone in my hand. I had decided to tell an African story that involved four different chants, and I had distributed copies of the chants beforehand — each on a different-colored sheet of paper. I would call out at the appropriate time, "Pink Papers," or "Green Papers," and those children with the right papers would provide the required response. I had not counted on the volume of the chanting, and the response was overwhelming. With thousands of children chanting and clapping on cue, the story took on the attributes of a ritual. As I was nearing the end, I looked up, and around the amphitheatre stood the circus people and animals — clowns, acrobats, elephants — all drawn by the chorus, watching the performance of the children, a setting by Fellini. For me, it was a powerful event, where reading aloud was completely embedded in story, and where story was alive and well, being lived at the moment by three thousand children.

## A REASON FOR READING ALOUD

Until the development of improvised drama, script was the natural factor relating drama and text. Unfortunately, it is also the most difficult of the reading activities, especially if the script is long or complex. The students have to penetrate someone else's written words and illuminate those words from their own experience. Then, using their memory, observation and perception, they have to invent complete characterizations, while remaining true to those suggested by the writer. They also have to memorize and deliver their lines to an audience, sounding as if they were creating the lines spontaneously. No easy task, even for a seasoned adult.

Much of the meaning of a play is in the subtext, which lies beneath the apparently logical order of the words in the text. In life, actions and words may seem to have an obvious and unambiguous meaning, but underneath there may be a whole range of motives and impulses that support or conflict with the obvious surface meaning.

By suggesting ideas, materials or methods, improvisation can give us reason for oral interpretation. Deeper understanding comes with the determination to grasp the whole of the text.

Text can be a starting point for improvisation, and improvisation may lead to a closer study and deeper understanding of the original text. Drama can be a means of releasing young children from "the tyranny of the script," allowing them to examine the themes within the printed text they have been given. Improvisation becomes a tool for the exploration of the ideas, relationships and language of the original text. It is important that much of the drama be not just the oral reading of a text, but a living through of its concepts.

I have found that reading aloud can be connected to drama in four ways: sharing rehearsed selections that may lead to dramatic exploration; reading aloud selections that have previously been the basis for dramatic exploration; reading aloud in role pieces within the drama (letters, proclamations, points of debate, songs and chants); and reflecting orally about the drama from personal journals, poems and related materials that may illuminate the work. Most children need assistance in working in an oral reading situation, and drama strategies have provided me with great support in this area.

Since few scripts for children are available (the writers of children's literature generally choose other genres), novels, poems and picture books written for children can be excellent sources of good dialogue that may easily be adapted for oral reading activities. Children can work in pairs or in small groups, reading the dialogue silently and then aloud. Teachers can have the children change roles; they can introduce new settings or new tensions; they can change the time period and use various other means to help children dramatize the selection in such a way that they can discover new meanings in it.

Readers Theatre is a technique for reading aloud stories and poems as if they were scripts. The actual words are used, and the narration, along with the dialogue, offers a set of exciting problems for children to explore. The simplest method is for some children to act as narrators while others read the bits of dialogue. When children begin to omit such lines as "he said" or "replied John," they are beginning to work with the interpretation of the meaning of the words, touching upon the sense of theatre that such an activity develops. However, there are dozens of options. For example, a character who speaks dialogue may also read the information or thoughts found in the narrative that refer to his/her role. Several characters can read narration as a chorus, or repeat lines as an echo or refrain. I am always amazed by the ingenuity of children when faced with making "out-loud" sense of a narrative selection. They see it as a puzzle, to be tried and treated until the whole picture is evident. With some physical arrangement, such as stools for the speakers, or a pool of light within which the group can work, Readers Theatre provides a perfect opportunity for oral interpretation, and a vehicle for dramatic exploration. The selection used for Readers Theatre can then be used within the drama work as a stimulus or source of tension that adds to the playmaking. The exercise of creating a Readers Theatre demonstration can serve as the beginning of the drama work, as the children build on events to create a frame for dramatic exploration.

In a unit on mining 100 years ago, for instance, court documents from a media box of related articles read aloud provided a powerful stimulus for continuing roleplay.

What children write from within the drama can serve as the basis for Readers Theatre with another group, either as an integral part of the work or as a reflective activity after the drama. Transcripts of improvised work, either tape recorded as the action takes place or recreated by scribes after the event, can help children to see the cause and effect of their roleplay, while providing materials for other groups to read aloud.

Children can read aloud findings from their research activities either to establish the context for the drama or within the work, feeding new strength and tension to the dramatic unit. Perhaps different groups have explored various aspects of a theme or topic, and need to hear from each other to expand their knowledge. They can transfer their findings to large charts or overhead transparencies and share the information, either in or out of role. Inside the drama structure, participants can read aloud documents, parables, lectures, excerpts, where the roleplay gives added strength to the belief and commitment in the work, often transcending any limitation or difficulty with bringing print to life. They can respond with the words of others to support their own ideas and viewpoints.

While in role, they can read aloud poems, songs, excerpts from novels and stories, or their own compositions, and can explore various interpretations of them. Working in small groups, children can select the interpretation they wish to give the words, and even devise ways to express the text in dramatic terms, establishing spatial relationships among the characters, and making specific recommendations (about tone, volume, pace) for how the words should be spoken.

In short, story drama can present text as "earprint." Some print longs to be said aloud, and we can bring words to the ears of our children in dozens of ways.

# 14

*Trusting the Sea People*
(Evaluating Growth in Story Drama)

The practical assessment of drama activities is not without problems. The various types of learning that occur in a drama program do not all lend themselves equally well to the assessment process. The teacher is attempting to assess the nature of an internal and personal process — of an inner experience — as well as to judge the external and public form. Since cognitive, affective and (at times) psychomotor learning occur simultaneously, it is a difficult task for the teacher to assess all the information that indicates learning in drama. An added difficulty is that assessment often needs to take place while the activities are in progress. Even though drama is a shared activity, individuals and their development are of fundamental importance. A drama experience is more than the sum of its parts; it requires an empathetic response from the teacher as well as an assessment of what has been learned. For example, the teacher could assess the drama of the class on the basis of the insights that have been gained, the extendings and elaborations of language that have occurred or the new understanding that a particular group has reached. If the teacher's intent in drama is to deepen the children's thinking, the impact of the work can be determined from the children's reactions. Their degree of involvement can be examined through the quality of their discussion, the intensity of their absorption in and awareness of role, and their range of language. An appreciation of the drama's outcome by the children — their ability to see the consequence of events — should also be recorded.

A class had been involved in a literature unit centred on the myths, poems and stories of selchies, mermaids and mermen. Drama work had been a major part of the three-week exploration but it had not taken place at set times. The activities had been stimulated by the children's reading; I as teacher had shaped the activities so that a variety of drama strategies could be used, and a range of assessments made possible.

The basic story, though there are many variations on it, is that there were once beautiful seal-women who left their skins on the shore while they sang and swam in the sea. A man, infatuated with them, stole one of the skins, and the seal-woman whose skin it was was forced to stay with him on shore for many years, bearing him children until one day she managed to find the skin and disappeared back into the sea forever.

These old tales are powerful, telling of transformation, spiritual as well as physical, loss as well as gain, heartbreak as well as love. The class of junior children I was working with had experienced several versions of the tale from my readings of picture books. During each session, we explored various aspects of the legend, and the student teachers and I began to collect data from observations both while we were inside the activities, and while we were distanced from the work as observers. By using this information, the teachers could develop a profile of assessment for each child, for the class as a community and for the teaching program itself.

The following record lists the strategies used in our work, the variety of activities that took place and assessment observations drawn from the teaching.

| Strategy | Activity | Assessment |
|---|---|---|
| Responding to a Story in Role | Working with *Greyling*, a story by Jane Yolen, the children created the village where a seal-boy lived. | Committing themselves to role. Building an environment. Identifying with drama context. |

| Strategy | Activity | Assessment |
|---|---|---|
| Exploring Ideas Alone and Unobserved | Each child, at the same time but working alone, explored the process of changing from a sea creature into a human. | Develop a character. Working autonomously. Accepting a role. |
| Improvisations in Groups | Each group created a scene where a selchie was first seen by villagers. | Moving in and out of role. Selecting and evaluating appropriately from the possibilities. Taking risks. |
| Interviewing Role | In each group, one reporter interviewed three villagers about sightings of sea people. | Small group work. Drawing on a variety of indirect experiences. Engaging in the drama. Revealing feelings in role. |
| Reporting on Events | Each reporter described the interview to the villagers to see if there were inaccuracies. | Reflecting on drama activity. Use of space. Sense of audience. Responding to ideas of others. |
| Depicting through Group Tableaux | The children retold the story by creating six group tableaux that depicted the incidents in it. | Sharing, valuing and responding to others. Connecting ideas. Staying on task. |
| Choral Speaking and Chanting | The villagers created a chant to call for help in ridding their village of sea creatures. | Interpreting text. Common artistic intentions. Reflecting upon emotional response. |

| Strategy | Activity | Assessment |
|---|---|---|
| Interpreting and Reading Aloud | The class was divided into groups to work on sections of a story. They used the convention of Readers' Theatre to interpret and retell the tale. | Interpreting the words of others. Collaborating and co-operating with others. Supporting contributions of others. |
| Play-making as a Class, Sharing and Appreciating Presentation | The class created a version of the story, built from their explorations in role, and shared it with a younger grade. | Shaping the work artistically. Establishing common artistic purposes. Gaining an overview of the work. Employing different functions of language. |
| Mapping and Graphing in Role | The children mapped out the island where the villagers lived, indicating the areas inhabited by sea creatures. | Reflecting on and reworking the drama. Recognizing implications of actions. Hypothesizing and brainstorming. |
| Making Masks and Storytelling | The children created masks of the sea people to wear in the final ritual of storytelling as a village. | Understanding the artform. Using various drama crafts. Awareness of dynamic of audience. |
| Singing in Role | The class learned the Selchie Song from the text and sang it. | Ensemble growth. Interpreting print sensitively. Maintaining mood. |
| Exploring through Sound and Dance Drama | The children created the sounds of the sea people to accompany a dance drama of a sea changeling being forced to leave the village against his will. | Creating a dramatic context. Working as part of an ensemble. Identifying with concerns of drama. |

| Strategy | Activity | Assessment |
| --- | --- | --- |
| Exploring with Mime | The children mimed putting on and taking off sealskins each day, and hiding them from humans. | Exploring and communicating non-verbally. Investigating possibilities. Viewing self as part of ensemble. |
| Games and Exercises | The class played "The Hidden Key" (a game where blindfolded players must catch another player who attempts to steal a key), as a prelude to the story of the changeling. | Co-operating through play. Working without teacher intervention. Interacting positively with others. |

As well, in this drama lesson the children used the strategy of "role on the wall" when they represented in picture form information necessary as the drama progressed. They traced each other's bodies on brown paper, then cut the tracings out. The figures formed skins that we first displayed then put into a pile, rolled up, bound with an elastic and hid. Suddenly the children's roles were distanced, but in a way the selchie quality was heightened. These skins were symbols of the drama and of the tension that lay at the heart of it. We need to hang our other selves on the wall once in a while in order to see what is underneath.

A good plan will help determine not only what you do, but how you evaluate the learning of each class. Of course, plans don't always work out, but sometimes there is unexpected learning you hadn't anticipated, and that can be just as exciting. And bear in mind that sometimes you don't have to insist on evaluating either yourself or the students: you can just enjoy a five-minute story drama break!

# And in Conclusion

### SHATTERING PORCELAIN IDEAS

"Where do you get your ideas?" That's the question most often asked of writers by non-writers. My ideas come from memories, images, dreams, stray happenings, but they all have one thing in common: I get the ideas because I was looking for ideas. A person who has it uppermost in his mind that someone is trying to poison him will often enough find that his food tastes a bit peculiar. The anticipation is all.

It was a cold winter. I was living alone in a house that was being torn down. Doors and window frames, stair landings, cabinets, siding and moldings were lying all about. Plaster littered the floor, and I kept warm by stoking the fireplace with scraps of wood, a sort of cannibalistic rite, the house consuming itself. I wondered about Humpty Dumpty one day. If he had been put back together by all the King's Horses and all the King's Men, could they ever have done it right? And if not — what? Also, after fourteen years of marriage, I was alone, my wife and children elsewhere. Broken up.

Richard Kennedy

I first read *The Porcelain Man* as a picture book, and when I subsequently found it in *Richard Kennedy: Collected Stories*, I realized that it was part of a significant body of work by a fine American writer. This is a startling story of loneliness and love, in which the author takes us into a fantasy that results in our seeing deeper into the human heart. A lonely girl living with her nasty father comes to build a man of porcelain, who tells her that he loves her. The twists and turns help us realize the difficulty of living with our choices in life. Eventually, the porcelain man is shattered, and his remains become a set of dishes. The story ends with the girl marrying another man, and at dinner, her porcelain plate says, ''I love you.'' I first heard the story told by my friend Bob Barton, a master storyteller. Now, whenever I read this narrative aloud, I hear Bob's voice whispering in my ear.

With a group of fifteen girls attending a summer camp, I began by reading the story *The Porcelain Man* as they sat in a semi-circle, with the teachers behind them looking on. In the ensuing discussion, the children were hesitant to participate, and I struggled with a variety of questions, attempting to find an entry point into the drama. I wanted to keep the group working as an ensemble for the first while, because of the visitors watching and their distrust of me as a guest. Eventually, we explored different thoughts about the talking plate, drawn from our memories of the story.

I presented a problem: the girls had to decide, as new brides, whether to sell or hide from their new husbands the dishes that could speak of love. Each girl discussed her views with one of the teachers who had been observing, now acting as a confidante. I roleplayed the husband, and asked the girls, one by one, in role as the wife, to tell me about the porcelain dishes that seemed so special to her. The girls then demonstrated their different approaches to the problem, from obliterating the porcelain plates to guarding them as hope for their future.

Some of the teachers worked in role as well, as neighbors who had borrowed the plate, or villagers who had heard stories from those who knew the girl from her past. One teacher wrote:

> Now David was ready to begin roleplaying as the husband, and tension was added by David in making the role of the husband harsh and narrow-minded. This tension helped the girls begin to believe in the drama.
>
> What stands out the most in my mind was my young partner's belief that if her new husband found out that the plate loved her, he would be crushed. The statement said so much to me. She understood the difference between a husband and a father, which many of the girls seemed not to understand. She was committed to protecting her husband. And the use of the word ''crushed''

gave me an image that she believed her husband was as fragile as the porcelain man.

To deepen the awareness of the dilemma, I explained that the husband had been called to war, and in role as that husband, I asked each of the girls in the circle, as my wife, to create a special meal on the porcelain plate to take with me. I had focused on one plate from the set that had demonstrated the ability to say, "I love you." How would each girl respond to my request to take the plate with me?

Discussion brought out a range of possibilities involving some deep thinking and problem solving that, from the tone of their voices and the expressions on their faces, the girls enjoyed. "Could she break something else and make another set (implying the power was in her rather than in the dish)." A "light bulb" moment for one of the girls was her suggestion to break the plate, mix it with other pieces of porcelain, and make two plates, one for him and one she could keep.

These wonderful beings came to us, in role, to debate the pros and cons of whether to keep the plate or give it to their husband. Stephanie is a very bright, verbal, independent young lady. I struggled to suppress my views of what she should do, resorting to comments and questions to find out how she felt in her heart. I found it fascinating, listening to her point of view since it was quite different from mine. Yes, she loved her husband, but she would not give up the plate. It had a special meaning to her, and she feared her husband would not understand. She could not put into words what this "special meaning" was, but from the look in her eyes, it was important and exciting to have something of their own. For a moment, I wondered, "Is this the age little girls have diaries and begin to lock them?" She liked sticking to her guns and being in opposition to her husband. Later, when in role, David asked her, "Do you know where the plate is?" she replied with a great deal of strength, "I broke it and didn't save the pieces."

The range of response from all the girls to this question revealed as much. "I'm not going to give it to you!" "I can't give it to you." "I think it might be..." "I'll look in the kitchen." "The plate is in the brook!" "I borrowed it." "And she broke it." Some were so strong and spoke out. For example when the girl said, "I have it but I won't give it to you." Or "I can't give it to you, what's in the past is not as special as the plate." Some felt strongly but had no voice. A little blonde girl, who had not spoken much, spontaneously mouthed, "My father gave it to me," to no one in particular while a stronger student was speaking out. I had not made that connection until I read her lips. The father had given the daughter the makings of the porcelain man.

To create an epilogue for the tale, the children worked in small groups, along with the teachers, to create silent scenes symbolic of the story's truth. To draw the session to a close, I returned to the opening scene as the children formed a circle with a teacher standing behind each girl, hands on shoulders, as an advisor, whispering suggestions and support, as I interviewed the girls who were each in role as the wife about whether they would choose to keep the plate in their new homes. While the teachers advised, the children responded with their own heartfelt ideas, often in contradiction to their advisors.

> David told us [the adults] that his goal in drama work is to reach an aesthetic moment that the children create, that they are in charge of. To me, this final moment in the drama with these girls was where it happened.
> I will do harder, tougher work.

These girls had formed their relationships before I had arrived in the school. Many of the teachers were greeted affectionately with hugs and kisses, and I knew that throughout the work, I would be the alien. Working in role as a catalyst was the first choice I made, and the children's ideas demonstrated intense thought and extreme confidence. The teachers were brave to let go of their immediate response of joining in with the spirit of collaboration in a camp-like setting, and help move the participants to another place and time. And the girls went with them, resulting in some powerful moments of drama. Making choices is what I do as a teacher, and the dynamics of the children, the space and the function of the lesson all drive me toward the rhythm of the work. Each teacher selects from a computer menu hidden deep within, and as we watch others making choices, we add to our own storehouse, knowing all the while we will never follow that schema again. Such is the unique quality of each teaching experience. In this case, we all chose to live in the drama, and I doubt any of us has forgotten that day.

So many concerns arose, and some of them still haunt me. When there are such powerful audiences for theatre, extravagant auditoria with computerized lighting boards, companies and artists from the world over sharing their talents, fifty years of drama educators nurturing and extending the techniques of the teachers, how will we as classroom teachers remember to listen to the tiniest children's voices hidden in the corners, to work with those young people who will never be on stage, to deepen the talents of those who feel they do not even need us?

My memories of teaching are captured in a notebook I keep, saved for my autumn days when I will need to look back. I remember the faces of the children, the voices of the teachers. Like children's books that exist only when a child is present, we only truly teach when the art and the child connect, so that for the moment, each of us, child and teacher, belongs to the "what if" world.

Dear Mr. Booth:

Thank you for coming and showing us that drama. I really enjoyed it! I thought that drama was only where you do plays, but you showed me that there is different kinds of drama. It was really good!

Yours truly,
Jennifer

# *Acknowledgments*

I want to thank four educators who have made a significant impact upon my teaching life:

Bill Moore, who was my supervisor of drama in Hamilton, Ontario, and who showed me the significance of the teacher in the classroom. He taught me that the respect of the child is the hallmark of this profession.

Richard Courtney from the Ontario Institute for Studies in Education in Toronto, who opened the doors of learning to me by demonstrating that teaching required a personal philosophy, and that by reading about and reflecting upon the work of other teachers and artists, we can come to find our own way.

Gavin Bolton from Durham University in England, who taught me the impact of reflection in my own work and the work of others. He pointed me towards the power of personal research in our particular artform.

Dorothy Heathcote from Newcastle University in England, who demonstrated for me that the search for truth within an artform is everything to the learner.

# *Publishing Acknowledgments*

I would like to thank the following for the kind permission to use excerpts from previously published writings:

The Ontario Ministry of Education, for excerpts from *Growing with Books*, and *The Ontario Assessment Instrument Pool*;

The Toronto Board of Education and Kathy Lundy for excerpts from *Drama Words*;

The Ohio State University for excerpts from *Theory into Practice*, Vol xxiv, #3, Summer 1985;

The Council of Drama in Education for excerpts from their Journal *Contact*;

Richard Kennedy and publisher, for the poem from "Oliver Hyde's Dishcloth Concert."

# References

Alexander, Lloyd. *The King's Fountain*. New York: Dutton, 1989.

Armitage, R. *The Trouble with Mr. Harris*. London: Andre Deutsch, 1979.

Barnes, Douglas. *From Communication to Curriculum*. Harmondsworth: Penguin, 1976.

Barton, Bob. *Tell Me Another*. Portsmouth, NH: Heinemann, 1986.

Bolton, Gavin. *New Perspectives on Classroom Drama*. Hemel Hempstead: Simon & Schuster, 1993.

Booth, David. *Classroom Voices*. Toronto/Tampa, Fl: Harcourt Brace, 1993.

Booth, David. *Dr. Knickerbocker and Other Rhymes*. Illustrated by Maryann Kovalski. Toronto: Kids Can Press, 1994.

Booth, David. *Drama Words: The Role of Drama in Language Growth*. Toronto: Language Study Centre, Toronto Board of Education, 1986.

Booth, David, and Bob Barton. *Stories in the Classroom*. Markham: Pembroke Publishers, 1990.

Braun, Willi. *The Expedition*.

Bruner, Jerome, et al. *Play: Its Development and Evolution*. Middlesex: Penguin, 1976.

Bulla, Clyde Robert. *Joseph the Dreamer*. New York: T.Y. Crowell, 1971.

Burningham, John. *Would You Rather...* London: Jonathan Cape, 1978.

Carrick, Donald. *Harald and the Giant Knight*. Clarion Books, 1982.

Chukovsky, K. *From Two to Five*. Berkeley: University of California Press, 1963.

Cooper, Susan. *The Selkie Girl*. New York: Atheneum, 1986.

Courtney, Richard. *Drama and Intelligence*. Montreal: McGill-Queen's University Press, 1990.

Courtney, Richard. *The Dramatic Curriculum*. New York: Drama Book Specialists, 1980.

Courtney, Richard. *Play, Drama and Thought*. Revised edition. Toronto: Simon & Pierre, 1991.

Gerstein, Mordecai. *The Seal Mother*. New York: Dial, 1986.

Goble, Paul. *The Iron Horse*. New York: Macmillan, 1984.

Hardy, Barbara. "Towards a Poetics of Fiction." In M. Meek, et al., eds., *The Cool Web*. London: The Bodley Head, 1977.

Heathcote, Dorothy. "Of These Seeds Becoming." In R. Shuman, *Educational Drama for Today's Schools*. Metuchen, NJ: The Scarecrow Press, 1978.

Hoban, Russell. *The Dancing Tigers*. London: Jonathan Cape, 1982.

Hyman, Trina Schart. *Snow White*. New York: Little, Brown, 1974.

Inglis, Fred. "Reading and Children's Novels." In G. Fox, *Writers, Critics and Children*. London: Heinemann, 1976.

Kennedy, Richard. "Oliver Hyde's Dishcloth Concert." In *Richard Kennedy: Collected Stories*. New York: Harper & Row, 1987.

Kennedy, Richard. "The Porcelain Man." In *Richard Kennedy: Collected Stories*. New York: Harper & Row, 1987.

Krueger, Kermit. *The Golden Swans*. London: Collins, 1970.

Lundy, Charles, and David Booth. *Interpretation: Working with Scripts*. Toronto: Harcourt, Brace, 1985.

Martin Jr., Bill, and John Archambault. *The Ghost-Eye Tree*. New York: Henry Holt & Company, 1985.

McConnell, Doc. "The Snake-Bit Hoe Handle." From *The Sounds of Language: First Grade to Eighth Grade*, Bill Martin Jr. Texas: DHM Publishers, 1990.

Moffett, James, and Betty Jane Wagner. *A Student-Centered Language Arts Curriculum*. Portsmouth, NH: Heinemann, 1992.

Morgan, Norah, and Julianna Saxton. *Teaching, Questioning and Learning*. London: Routledge & Kegan Paul, 1991.

Neelands, Jonothan. *Structuring Drama Work*. Tony Goode, ed. Cambridge: Cambridge University Press, 1990.

Neelands, Jonothan, David Booth, Suzanne Ziegler. *Writing in Imagined Contexts: Research into Drama-Influenced Writing.* Toronto: Toronto Board of Education, 1993.

O'Brien, Robert. *Mrs. Frisby and the Rats of NIMH.* Atheneum, 1971.

O'Neill, Cecily, and Allan Lambert. *Drama Structures.* London: Hutchinson, 1982.

Paley, Vivian Gussin. *The Boy Who Would Be a Helicopter.* Cambridge, Ma: Harvard University Press, 1990.

Paulsen, Gary. *The Monument.* New York: Delacorte Press, 1991.

Ross, Ramon. *Storyteller.* Charles E. Merrill, 1980.

Rosen, Harold. *Stories and their Meanings.* London: National Association for the Teaching of English.

Wells, Gordon. *The Meaning Makers.* Portsmouth, NH: Heinemann, 1986.

Wolkstein, Diane. *The Red Lion.* New York: Schocken, 1980.

Woolland, Brian. *The Teaching of Drama in the Primary School.* London: Longman, 1993.

Yee, Paul. "Rider Chan." In *Tales From Gold Mountain.* Toronto: Groundwood, 1989.

Yee, Paul. "Spirits of the Railway." In *Tales From Gold Mountain.* Toronto: Groundwood, 1989.

Yep, Laurence. *The Rainbow People.* Harper & Row, 1989.

Yolen, Jane. *Children of the Wolf.* The Viking Press, 1984.

Yolen, Jane. *Greyling.* Philomel Books, 1991.

Young, Ed. *Lon Po Po: A Red-Riding Hood Story from China.* Philomel Books, 1989.

Zavrel, S. *Vodnik.* London: Abelard-Schuman, 1970.

(have my (inside) change)

If you could change one
thing in this school,
what would it be?

to an
"special"

(what message would you
send) (by pigeon)?

- homing pigeon...
- decode or message